Embracing Your Inner Child

A Journey to Self-Healing and Emotional Freedom

Ellie Bloom

Contents

Introduction

♥

Hey there,

Ever felt that nostalgic tug at your heart, reminding you of a time when life was simpler, and joy flowed effortlessly? Well, that's your inner child waving hello from the quiet corners of your heart! I'm here to invite you on a special expedition—an adventure of self-discovery and healing.

In our time together, we'll skip the jargon and opt for practical exercises and therapeutic techniques. No rigid rules here—think of it as an open invitation to witness the magic of self-love, compassion, and finding yourself.

This journey isn't about reaching a fixed destination; it's about unfolding your authentic self. Consider this more than just a book—it's your compass, guiding you back to the heart of who you truly are.

So, let's embark on this sacred expedition together. Think of it as a sanctuary for your soul, a tapestry woven with threads of resilience and hope. Welcome to the journey of a lifetime—welcome to embracing your inner child. Get ready for something special!

The Inner Child Explained

♥

"Within every adult, there is a child crying for help. We are that child, and the healing process begins with our willingness to nurture that inner child." - Thich Nhat Hanh

What is the Inner Child?

Ready to dive into this transformative journey with me? Picture your inner child as your own personal time capsule, holding onto the pure, unfiltered memories of your early adventures—the sweet and the bitter moments. It's that genuine, unfiltered version of yourself before adulting threw in its curveballs.

Think of your inner child as your trusty sidekick—small, curious, and filled with raw emotions. Like a tiny seed promising growth and transformation, your inner child is a fundamental part of what makes you unique. The tricky part? Life's twists and turns often lead us to unintentionally neglect or harm this vital part of ourselves.

Psychologically speaking, the inner child is like a symbol, carrying the emotional memories and responses formed during those childhood years. It's the lens through which we see the world, shaped by the rollercoaster of joys, sorrows, and insecurities during our formative years.

Imagine your emotional memory as a garden, with your inner child as the guardian. Early experiences, both good and not-so-great, are like seeds planted in this garden. Your inner child nurtures them, influencing how you see things, build relationships, and react emotionally in adulthood. Embracing your inner child is like unlocking the gate to this garden, gaining insight into the roots of your emotional landscape.

Fyodor Dostoevsky once said, "The soul is healed by being with children."

The Inner Child in Everyday Life

In the chaos of adulting, the inner child often gets neglected. You know, that part of us that holds onto the memories of our early adventures—the good, the not-so-good, the whole shebang. Turns out, those unattended wounds from the past can sneakily influence our present, messing with our relationships, self-perception, and overall emotional vibe.

Before you think this is a trip back in time, consider this is an invitation to connect with your true self. Think of it as giving a little love to that vulnerable part of you. This inner child work thing? It's like gently digging up buried emotions, becoming your own superhero, and building a foundation of resilience and self-love.

So, how does this inner child thing sneak into our everyday? Picture it like a quiet puppet master, pulling the strings of our behaviors and choices. Ever find yourself having a big emotional reaction that doesn't quite match the situation? Yeah, that might be your inner child nudging you with some unresolved stuff from way back when.

And it's not just in those emotional rollercoasters; it plays a part in the choices we make in relationships, careers, and life goals. Seeking validation, fearing rejection, or dodging vulnerability? All road signs from your inner child trying to navigate the early relational maze.

To unravel this, take a moment to reflect. When things get intense, check if your emotional reactions feel a bit out of proportion. Notice any recurring patterns in your behavior? Those might have roots in your past experiences. And relationships, oh boy—do you spot any trust issues, fear of abandonment, or struggles with vulnerability? Your inner child might be trying to tell you something there.

What about comfort zones and fears? Anything that triggers a strong emotional response? Dive into the origins. And those moments of pure joy? The things that make you smile? Yeah, that's your inner child's sweet spot.

Okay, now let's get real. Pay attention to your inner dialogue. Is it a harsh critic or a supportive buddy? And creativity and play—do you embrace them with the same enthusiasm as your inner child would?

Here are some of the questions to ponder as we venture on this journey together:

- Ever feel like your emotional reactions are a bit much for the situation, echoing childhood feelings?

- Spot any recurring patterns in your adult behavior that might have roots in your early years?

- How about relationships—any themes like trust issues or struggles with vulnerability?

- What triggers strong emotional responses in your life, and do they connect to your past?

- Think about the activities that genuinely bring joy to your face—are they in line with your inner child's interests?

- Check your inner dialogue during self-reflection—harsh critic or nurturing friend?

- Are you still rocking the imaginative and playful vibe in your creative pursuits?

- And lastly, those dreams—any recurring themes that connect to your early memories?

These questions are like guideposts, helping you explore the intricate landscape of your inner child. Take this journey with patience and curiosity, and let the whispers of your past light the way to self-discovery and healing.

The Impact of Childhood Experiences

We're kicking off with a peek into how our childhood experiences pull the strings on our emotional landscapes. Every high-five, every tough moment, they're like brushstrokes on the canvas of our grown-up selves.

Good childhood vibes? They're like the sunshine that helps our inner child grow resilient. Whether it's the warmth of loving relationships, encouragement from our folks, or just diving into some creative fun—these moments build a secure and confident foundation. It's the emotional nutrients our inner child needs to blossom into a self-assured adult with healthy relationships.

Now, the things that are less wonderful—negative experiences cast shadows that linger. Trauma, neglect, or tough environments can mess with the healthy development of our emotional resilience, leaving scars that stick around into adulthood. Those unresolved childhood wounds might show up as struggles in forming secure connections, dealing with stress, or handling emotions like a pro.

Ever heard of attachment theory? It's like the compass of our emotional journey, exploring the bonds between kiddos and their main caregivers. Secure attachments in infancy become the bedrock of a resilient inner child. They're like the VIP pass to exploring the world confidently, forming solid relationships, and rocking emotional resilience throughout life.

But, if those attachments are a bit wonky, it can lead to a bumpy ride in adulthood. Think intimacy struggles, trust issues, and a dip in self-worth. Turns out, the impact of early bonding experiences with our inner child sticks around.

Now, let's chat about some psychology legends—Erik Erikson and Jean Piaget. They shine a light on the stages of our mental and emotional growth. Erikson's "Trust vs. Mistrust" stage in infancy? It's like the planting grounds for trust or mistrust, based on the quality of caregiving. Positive experiences here lay the groundwork for a resilient inner child, while inconsistency or neglect can breed mistrust.

Piaget's "Sensorimotor Stage" is all about early stimuli shaping cognitive development. Responsive caregiving during this stage supports our inner child's curiosity and exploration, while a lack of stimulation can slow down cognitive growth.

Social skills? They get a spotlight during Erikson's "Initiative vs. Guilt" stage. Positive interactions contribute to healthy interpersonal skills, but criticism or restrictions can hinder social development, affecting our inner child's ability to navigate relationships.

And let's not forget personality. Both Erikson and Piaget say early experiences leave a mark on personality development. Positive reinforcement during those formative years builds resilience, while criticism or negativity might give rise to self-doubt.

People who grew up in positive, nurturing environments tend to rock greater emotional resilience, academic success, and a satisfying life overall. On the flip side, those with rough childhoods, like abuse or neglect, might face a higher risk of mental health challenges, substance abuse, and health issues in adulthood.

On the flip side, Adverse Childhood Experiences (ACEs) can bring on mental health challenges, substance abuse, and adverse physical health impacts. Childhood experiences even shape adult relationships, with ACEs linked to difficulties in trust, intimacy, and communication.

So, what's the takeaway? It's high time we prioritize positive childhood experiences and tackle the not-so-great events for the long-term well-being of everyone. Bring in a compassionate and comprehensive approach, acknowledging both the positive and negative influences. That way, we're paving the way for a healing journey that nurtures resilience, fosters emotional well-being, and empowers the inner child to thrive despite the shadows of the past.

Recognizing Inner Child Wounds

Let's discuss something that might feel a bit deep but is super important—the wounds that our inner child might be carrying. Think of it as a gentle exploration into the emotional imprints that shape how we see the world, affect our relationships, and play a role in our overall well-being.

First things first, we've got to identify these wounds to kickstart the journey toward emotional liberation and self-restoration. They're like emotional scars, imprints left by experiences that run deep. We're talking about the lingering impact of abandonment, neglect, or the echoes of physical and emotional abuse. Feelings of inadequacy, whether from comparisons or unmet needs, can also leave their mark. Each wound forms a unique pattern that shapes how we see and react to the world. Understanding these wounds is like cracking the emotional code, helping us navigate targeted healing and creating a space where the wounded inner child can find its voice and solace in compassion.

There are some childhood wounds that are, unfortunately, all too common. Things we might've carried from childhood—the kind of wounds that linger. Ever felt neglected or abandoned? That's the abandonment vibe. Been through experiences where you felt not accepted or valued? That's the rejection story. Did trust get shattered in some significant relationships? Hello, betrayal. And that deep-seated feeling of unworthiness and self-blame? That's shame knocking on the door. Recognizing these vibes is like shining a light on what might be affecting us today.

But how do we know if these wounds are still hanging around? Well, repressed emotions are like tangible evidence, showing unprocessed feelings from childhood that lurk beneath the surface, affecting our adult lives. Those stifled emotions tend to resurface in unexpected ways, triggered by events resembling the circumstances in which they were suppressed. This emotional dance significantly influences our reactions, decisions, and overall well-being, highlighting the intricate nature of our emotional landscape.

Recognizing these echoes of repressed emotions isn't just about understanding where they come from—it's a vital step in breaking free from their hold. Research shows that acknowledging and understanding the origins of these emotions lays the foundation for a transformative journey toward emotional liberation and a more authentic life.

So, how do we start this journey? Let's shine a light on our inner landscape with these self-assessment tools:

Journaling Prompts: Reflect on memories, life events, and recurring patterns by asking yourself questions like, "What childhood memories still stir strong emotions?" or "Are there consistent themes in my reactions to certain situations?"

Emotional Checklists: Keep tabs on your emotional state throughout the day using checklists. Note down feelings regularly to identify patterns and recurring emotions.

Therapeutic Guidance: Connect with a qualified therapist or counselor. Their support provides a safe space to explore and process past experiences, offering effective strategies for healing.

Visualization Exercises: Take a trip back in time with visualization. Picture yourself at different stages of childhood, noting any emotional reactions or memories that pop up. It's a powerful tool for unearthing buried emotions and recognizing wounds that need attention.

Recognizing inner child wounds is a journey that calls for courage and self-reflection. By using these tools, you're stepping into a space of self-discovery, gaining clarity on wounds that might be influencing your present experiences, and laying the foundation for healing and growth.

Healing vs. Suppressing

Picture it. You're here, reading to dive into your inner child work, standing at a crossroads, right? You have a fundamental choice: either dive into healing or take the road of suppression. Let's break down these approaches, so you can figure out which path feels right for you.

Healing that inner child is like a conscious and compassionate dance with your past wounds. It's about facing those emotions and traumas that might have been pushed aside during childhood. Imagine it as a transformative process where you become your own loving parent, embracing the inner child's needs with understanding. By doing this, you're basically unlocking the door to profound healing. It's like shedding the weight of emotional baggage and opening up the way for some genuine self-discovery.

On the other hand, there's suppressing the inner child. It's like putting its needs on the back burner, maybe as a way to deal with the complexities of adulting. Sure, it might temporarily numb the pain, but it comes with a hefty cost. Ignoring the inner child can lead to a disconnection from your authentic self, leaving you feeling kinda empty or unfulfilled. Over time, this neglect can show up as anxiety, depression, or struggles in forming meaningful connections. Those unaddressed wounds might stick around, pulling the strings on your behaviors, relationships, and overall satisfaction with life.

Now, let's dive into some real-life stories that shout out the triumph of healing over suppression. First up, we've got Sarah—a true artist rediscovering her passion for painting. In childhood, her creativity and artistic pursuits were stifled. She found herself in a life of rigid structure that felt unnatural. As she embraced her inner child's creativity, the healing journey unfolded. Imagine each stroke of the brush as a conversation with her younger self, bringing back the joy buried beneath layers of societal conditioning. Sarah didn't just paint canvases; she painted a whole new narrative infused with authenticity, joy, and the freedom to embrace passions without holding back.

Then there's Alex, on a journey of self-love that's nothing short of inspiring. As Alex explored childhood experiences, the roots of persistent self-doubt started to unravel. With a past of inconsistent parenting and insecure attachments, childhood was not an easy feat. Through therapy, Alex dismantled the critical narrative, replacing it with self-compassion and acceptance. Post-healing, Alex found this deep connection between childhood experiences and adult self-perception. The inner critic transformed into an inner ally, paving the way for a narrative marked by resilience, authenticity, and a strong belief in personal worth.

These stories are like little roadmaps, showing how healing that inner child unravels the complexities of our narratives. It's all about that profound transformation and emotional freedom. As you flip the page, remember, that the journey has just begun. The inner child's got secrets to share, unveiling the roadmap to self-healing and emotional freedom. Ready for the next chapter? Let's go!

Communicating with Your Inner Child

Initiating the Dialogue

So, we're stepping into this sacred space where the present meets the past, and the first steps toward healing start with a gentle initiation of a dialogue with your inner child. It's like sitting down with the younger version of yourself and giving a listen to those whispers that have been tucked away for so long.

Now, I get it. This journey might feel like a leap into the unknown but fear not. Find a cozy spot where you can connect with your inner child without any distractions. Close your eyes, take a deep breath, and picture a warm, inviting space. Extend your hand with kindness and understanding, inviting your inner child to join you in this cozy mental hangout.

Remember, initiating and maintaining this dialogue is like chatting with an old, beloved friend. Start by speaking to the innermost part of yourself with just a few simple words: "I am here for you, and I am ready to listen." "Your feelings are valid, and I honor them." "Together, we embark on a journey of healing and understanding."

Once you are ready to start talking to your inner child, journaling can act as a powerful tool to deepen the conversation—it's like the parchment where the stories of your inner child unfold. Try these prompts as a gentle way to begin unlocking the narrative:

- Take a stroll down memory lane—both the good and not-so-great parts—and explore the emotions they stir up today.

- Dig into those childhood passions—see if they're still part of your life and spill any unfulfilled desires or dreams from back in the day.

- Have a heart-to-heart with your younger self—ask about dreams, fears, and needs. Respond from your present perspective and channel that nurturing parent vibe.

- Keep an eye on situations triggering strong emotions—reflect on how they might connect to past experiences and think about how your inner child would see and react to these triggers.

- Recognize your childhood strengths—consider if these awesome traits are still kickin' in your adult life and how embracing them can support your inner child's well-being.

If journaling isn't for you or you want to try another approach, meditation is like a cozy date with your inner child. Picture this: imagine your younger self in a space that feels like a warm hug, doing things that light up their world. It could be playing, drawing, or just chilling in their favorite spot.

Now, close your eyes, take a deep breath, and let's do a little body scan. Feel any tension or knots? Yeah, those are like little whispers from your inner child. Focus on those areas, and send some good vibes their way—imagine warmth and comfort seeping into those spots. It's like giving your inner child a big, comforting hug.

Next up, pick a symbol that represents your inner child. It could be anything—a favorite toy, a special place, or even a color or a smell that feels just right. Now, take that symbol on a little journey during meditation. Imagine it leading you through memories and experiences, unlocking the doors to your inner child's world. It's like stepping into a treasure trove of emotions and rediscovering the magic that's always been there.

There's light—warm, nurturing light. Picture it surrounding you, wrapping you up like a protective blanket. Let it gently seep into your being, bringing not just warmth but healing vibes to your inner child. It's like a soft embrace that says, "Hey, I'm here for you, bringing comfort, love, and a bit of magic."

So, whether you're visualizing that safe and cozy space, doing a body scan, taking your inner child on a symbolic journey, or bathing in that warm, nurturing light, it's all about creating a space where your inner child feels heard, understood, and loved. Let the imagination flow, and let the healing vibes roll! You got this.

These practices are like secret passages to deeper self-discovery and communication with your inner child. Let them unfold naturally, creating a space for healing and connection. As you dive into this journey of introspection, remember that the insights gained from these practices are stepping stones toward a more profound understanding of your inner child's needs and desires. Embrace the process with patience and compassion, nurturing the bond with your inner child and laying the groundwork for transformative healing and self-discovery.

And how do you keep this conversation going? Make it a habit to check in with your inner child daily. Ask about their emotions, concerns, or joys—build that ongoing and evolving dialogue. Mindfulness practices are also your buddies here. By being aware of your thoughts and emotions without judgment, you create space for the natural surfacing of your inner child's voice. Oh, and throw in some affirmations and reassurance. Repeat positive statements like "I am here for you" or "You are safe and loved." They act like a consistent source of comfort, strengthening the connection and ensuring a nurturing and supportive inner dialogue.

Remember, starting and maintaining this inner dialogue is a chill, gradual process. Be patient and gentle with yourself, allowing the conversation to unfold naturally over time. The key is to create a space of trust and openness, fostering a relationship with your inner child built on understanding and compassion.

Understanding Your Inner Child's Language

Now, something super intriguing – the language of your inner child. It's not all words and sentences; think of it as this gentle symphony playing in the background of your soul. Understanding this language is like finding the key to a treasure chest full of profound messages hidden in your experiences.

So, emotions are like messengers from your inner child. When you're feeling sad, it's like a little nudge saying, "Hey, I've got something to share." Instead of brushing it off, why not ask gently, "What's the story behind this feeling?" And behaviors, they're not just random actions; they're your inner child's way of sending messages, like a plea for you to notice and understand.

Now, let's decode this emotional and behavioral language together.

Ever notice situations that trigger strong emotions? Those are like neon signs from your inner child, pointing to unmet needs or past wounds. Take a moment to dig into the origins of these triggers.

And if certain emotions pop up in the same situations over and over, your inner child might be dropping hints. For example, feeling abandoned during separations – that could be an unhealed inner child wound knocking on the door. Sometimes emotions go full-on fireworks mode, right? When they feel way too intense for the situation, it's like your inner child saying, "Hey, there's more to this." Investigate why those emotions are cranked up and check if they link back to your inner child's history.

Oh, and grab yourself a journal! Describe what you felt in specific situations and dig into any connections to your past. Journaling is like turning on the spotlight, revealing the hidden messages within your emotional landscape. It's something that you can go back to again and again.

Now, let's talk about behaviors. Notice any recurring behaviors or habits? Those could be messages from your inner child, trying to tell you something important. Take a closer look and find out what they're trying to say. Why do you do what you do? Seeking approval like it's a mission? That could be your inner child shouting, "I need acknowledgment!"

Reflect on your childhood coping strategies. If your adult behaviors mimic those childhood tactics, it's like your inner child saying, "Remember me? I still need attention." Recognizing these connections is key to understanding the messages behind your behaviors.

As you dive into the dance with your inner child, remember – patience is your best friend. Be gentle with yourself because understanding this language is a journey that takes time and kindness. Every revelation is a step closer to a more profound connection with your inner child. So, here's to self-awareness, healing, and a whole lot of compassion!

Responding to Your Inner Child

Learning to respond to your inner child is the cornerstone of this incredible journey toward healing. So, buckle up as we explore techniques that are all about nurturing, comforting, and giving your younger self some serious love.

When your inner child speaks up, responding with care is key to building that healing connection. One fun and simple technique is using positive affirmations that speak directly to your inner child's needs. If feelings of not being good enough pop up, throw an affirmation their way, like "You are worthy and deserving of love." Another move is visualization – picture yourself giving your inner child a big, comforting hug during vulnerable moments. It creates this safe mental space, reinforcing the security your inner child craves. And let's not forget the power of self-compassion– treat your own struggles with kindness, just like you would for a distressed child. I understand that this is easier said than done, but responding to your inner child is an ongoing chat filled with love and understanding, creating the perfect environment for emotional growth and resilience. Be nice to yourself. And be patient!

Now, how about some scripts to affirm and comfort your inner child through the good, the bad, and the ugly moments? Some of them might sound corny at first, but trust the process. Say it to your inner child, inwardly, gently, and genuinely. I bet you will feel something warm and fuzzy.

If your inner child says, "I feel like I'm not good enough," you can say, "Hey there, sweet one. You are inherently worthy and deserving of love. Your uniqueness adds beauty to the world, and I cherish every part of you. Together, we'll navigate through any doubts, and I'm here to remind you of your value."

And if feelings of fear or anxiety appear, your response could be, "It's okay, my little friend. I see your fear, and I'm here to keep you safe. Take a deep breath; you are protected, and I'll stand by you. Together, we'll create a space of security and calmness."

For those moments when your inner child questions their lovability, you can say, "Oh, my dear one, you are so lovable just as you are. There's nothing you need to change or prove to be worthy of love. I love you unconditionally, and I'm here to shower you with the love you deserve. Embrace it; you are cherished."

And when they're feeling sad and alone, your response might be, "I hear you, and I'm here. Your sadness is valid, and you're not alone anymore. Let's sit together, feel those emotions, and know that you are held in a warm embrace of understanding and compassion. We'll get through this together."

Lastly, for those overwhelming moments, you can say, "I understand, my precious one. When life feels overwhelming, remember that I'm here to support you. Let's take it one step at a time, and I'll guide you through. You are not alone, and together, we'll find calm in the chaos."

These scripts are like personalized notes for your inner child – use them to respond to their unique needs and emotions and tailor them to fit your style. Write them on your bathroom mirror, stick a note on the fridge; consistent affirmations and comfort build the foundation for a nurturing relationship with your inner child.

There is so much more you can do for your inner child outside of just words though. Why not indulge in playful self-care rituals? Engage in activities that bring back those childhood giggles – coloring, dancing, or playing a favorite game. It's like letting your inner child feel carefree and cherished all over again. Encourage self-expression! Let out that creative side by keeping a journal, doodling, or expressing yourself through art.

Also, establish gratitude rituals where you acknowledge and celebrate small victories and moments of joy. All too often, we forget to appreciate ourselves and how beautiful we are. Cultivate a habit of gentle and comforting self-talk. When faced with challenges, offer words of encouragement, acknowledging your inner child's emotions and providing reassurance that you are there to navigate difficulties together.

Express gratitude directly to your inner child for their resilience and strengths – this will reinforce the connection you're cultivating with your inner child and foster a safe space.

Building a Relationship

Think of it as a dynamic relationship that, just like any other, demands dedication and your consistent presence to truly flourish. Imagine regular check-ins – those moments when you're fully there, offering emotional support and connection. That's the secret sauce to keep this special bond thriving. Just like the undivided attention you expect from a friend or loved one when you are sharing, give yourself the space to provide that same undivided attention to your inner child.

Sometimes, scheduled reflections can be a total game-changer. Setting aside deliberate moments for this sacred dialogue with your inner child allows you to consciously take this journey and be mentally prepared to navigate your inner terrain. You could even create a little ritual to kick off these reflective sessions. Like a special handshake, setting the stage for a consistent and reassuring environment. Your inner child gets to know that you've got their back, no matter what.

We all know that schedules don't always stick and sometimes life gets in the way. So consider thinking of activities and affirmations specifically designed to wrap your inner child in comfort and reassurance when life gets a bit tricky. It can be something simple like taking a moment to yourself to listen to a special song or just quietly sip your coffee and doodle on a napkin. Whatever works for you, it's like having a structured framework for emotional care, a trusty toolkit for your inner child. Picture it as creating a safety net, reinforcing the sense of safety and trust within this unique relationship.

So, in this wild adventure of healing, remember: your inner child craves reliability. Envision a bond that's as strong as your morning coffee routine – consistently there, offering unwavering support. It's a journey, and you've got a trusty companion in your inner child every step of the way.

Nurturing Through Creativity

Unleashing the magic of creative expression as a powerful tool to nurture your inner child. Creative outlets are not just hobbies; they're like secret passages to connect with the little you inside. So, what's on the menu? Picture yourself with a canvas and a splash of colors, or maybe grooving to your favorite tunes. It's like a playdate with your inner child, a chance to let those emotions out in the most vibrant and freeing ways. Trust me, your inner child is ready to dance, paint, or sing its heart out, and you're just the right guide for this imaginative journey!

Now, let's dive into the playground of possibilities. Ever tried expressing yourself through art? Grab a paintbrush, draw, or sculpt – it's like having a direct conversation with your inner child's feelings. Dance is another fantastic playground; let those emotions flow through your body, whether it's a happy jig or a contemplative sway. And then, there's the enchanting world of music – create playlists that speak to your inner child's emotions. As the melodies play, you're not just listening; you're decoding the messages from your past. These creative outlets are not just activities; they're like love letters to your inner child, saying, "Hey, I'm here, and we're in this together. Let's have fun!"

So, grab that canvas, put on your favorite song, or just dance like no one's watching. Your inner child is throwing a party, and you're the VIP guest. It's not just about being creative; it's about connecting, laughing, and maybe shedding a few happy tears with the little you who's been waiting for this moment.

Let me share a couple of stories that might resonate with you:

Meet Emma, a resilient thirty-something with an unwavering spirit, embarking on a journey to heal her inner child. Growing up in a small town, Emma faced the challenge of navigating a tumultuous family environment, where the echoes of harsh words and unmet needs left an indelible mark on her self-worth. Struggling with feelings of unworthiness and a sense of not being seen, Emma sought solace in her passion for art. Turning to painting, she found refuge in a makeshift studio in her cozy apartment. The smell of acrylics, the touch of the brush against canvas – it all became a therapeutic dance for Emma. As she explored vibrant colors and fluid strokes, each piece of art became a conversation with her younger self, a visual narrative that gradually mended the wounds of her past. Through this creative process, Emma not only discovered healing but also unearthed a newfound sense of empowerment and authenticity, like a blooming flower breaking through the cracks in the pavement.

Now, let's delve into Mark's story, a guy with a heart as big as his love for dance. Raised in a bustling city, Mark's childhood was colored by emotional neglect, the subtle but profound absence of the warmth he craved. The weight of unspoken emotions lingered as he navigated through adolescence and into adulthood. Mark's connection with dance didn't start with grand stages or formal training; it began in the living room of his apartment. Picture Mark surrounded by eclectic musical playlists – a mix of genres that mirrored the symphony of emotions within. In those beats, he found a language for his inner child, a way to express the joy, pain, and everything in between. Each movement became a story, unraveling layers of emotional baggage he hadn't fully explored. Dancing in the privacy of his home, Mark discovered a newfound freedom that transcended the constraints of spoken language. It was a journey that transformed his relationship with himself, bridging the gap between the child who longed for recognition and the adult finding joy in the rhythm of life.

So, as you turn the pages ahead, let these tools and stories be your companions. The dialogue with your inner child is a dance – a beautiful choreography of healing and understanding.

Healing Inner Child Wounds

♥

Identifying and Acknowledging Pain

Now for the hard part: discovering the art of acknowledging and navigating through the complexities of pain in our lives. Think of it as gently unraveling threads in the intricate tapestry of your unique story, where moments of discomfort and sadness are woven with threads of joy. It's a courageous act that involves exploring the canvas of your inner child, and the journey towards healing begins by creating a safe space – one that's judgment-free and allows you to proceed at your own pace.

Take a moment to reflect on your past, those moments that might bring up some uneasy feelings. It's not about dwelling in the past but about freeing your present from the weight of unresolved emotions. Let these memories surface without fear, embracing them with an open heart. Trust me, it's within this safe acknowledgment that the magic of healing truly begins. Allow yourself the grace to explore these memories, knowing that each step forward is a step towards liberating your present self from the shackles of the past.

Validation is the soothing balm for your inner child's wounds. As you acknowledge the emotions tied to those past experiences, recognize the validity of your younger self's feelings. Don't shy away from the uncomfortable realities that may surface. Embrace self-compassion, understanding that your inner child did their best with the tools they had at the time. Treat yourself with the kindness and understanding you would offer to a true friend. This self-compassion transforms acknowledgment into healing, paving the way for the beautiful journey of re-parenting that lies ahead.

As you validate your emotions, you're creating a nurturing environment where your inner child's wounds can mend, bringing forth a renewed sense of self-love and acceptance. It's a powerful journey, and you're not alone in it. We're navigating it together.

Re-Parenting Yourself

Re-parenting is like stepping into the shoes of a loving and compassionate parent for your younger self, offering care, understanding, and validation that might've been missed. This isn't just a therapeutic technique; it's a soulful adventure, and a conscious choice to rewrite your inner story. None of our childhood's were perfect, this is an opportunity to fill in the gaps of that imperfection on your own, as the strong adult that you now are.

Embarking on this journey of re-parenting is all about patience, empathy, and a gentle touch. By tuning into the unmet needs and yearnings of your inner child, addressing them with the tenderness they might've missed out on; by imagining intentional acts of self-care, positive affirmations, and nurturing self-talk – you take the reins of your healing journey. It's a sacred promise to be there for yourself, offering the unwavering support and encouragement of those inner child cravings.

So, how can you show up for yourself in this way? Well, nurturing rituals are one fantastic tool. Whether it's a cozy bath, a comforting cup of tea, or just some quality alone time – these intentional acts are a simple way to show love towards yourself and show your inner child that their needs are not just noticed but deeply valued.

Daily affirmations are also a total game-changer – start your day with statements affirming your worth, capabilities, and inherent value. They're like gentle little reminders of your intrinsic worthiness, pushing aside any lingering self-doubt or negative perceptions. Develop a way of speaking to yourself that mirrors the tone of a caring and wise mentor. This way, you can act as an ongoing source of reassurance, offering guidance and support to your inner child as they navigate life's twists and turns.

As you wholeheartedly step into the re-parenting journey, let's first discuss something crucial – the 'Good Enough' parent model. Your parents weren't perfect; mine weren't either. So, let's drop that heavy expectation of perfection, especially on ourselves. The 'Good Enough' parent model is like a wise friend, nudging us to embrace the reality that perfection is simply unrealistic.

Now, here's the magical and most difficult part – internalize the ethos of the 'Good Enough' parent within yourself. It's about offering love and guidance without the crushing weight of unattainable expectations. Remember, mistakes are not roadblocks; they're stepping stones in this transformative process. Allowing yourself grace is a key part of the re-parenting journey. It's like saying, "Hey, I'm doing my best, and that's pretty good!"

Think of it as a gentle reminder that parenting, even when it's self-parenting, is a learning curve. You're navigating uncharted waters, figuring things out as you go. The 'Good Enough' parent model encourages a balanced approach – nurturing and creating space for growth without the burden of perfection. So, take a deep breath, embrace imperfections, and continue this journey with a heart full of compassion and understanding.

Forgiving the Past

Forgiveness is a key player in the ongoing journey of healing your inner child. It's like a compass guiding you through this transformative process of liberating yourself from the shackles of resentment. And guess what? It's not just about letting go; it's about opening doors to profound healing. So, grab a cup of something comforting, and let's dive into some forgiveness exercises together – your toolkit for this journey.

First, we need to reflect and understand. Picture this as unraveling the roots of resentment. It's not about saying what happened is okay; it's about liberating yourself from the emotional burden it carries. Try writing exercises – articulate those feelings, give them a voice, and let clarity be your guide. Imagine the situation, the person, and the emotions that you are holding onto. Write it all down and then read it back to yourself. Is this a feeling that you want to continue carrying with you? Why has it been so difficult for you to forgive up to this point? How do you think the other person feels about the situation?

Empathy practice is a bit like slipping into someone else's shoes. Now, let's be real – it's not the easiest thing to do, but it's absolutely necessary. It's like a powerful tool in your kit for understanding others and, ultimately, yourself. And here's the deal: it's definitely not about justifying their actions, not in the slightest. We're not here to make excuses or brush things under the rug. It's about diving into the complexities of what it means to be human in this world.

Think about it – we all carry our own set of wounds, some visible, some hidden deep within. Those wounds, they play a significant role in shaping how we show up in the world. And guess what? It's not always intentional. People act in ways they don't even realize, influenced by their own struggles and experiences.

So, when you're practicing empathy, it's not about saying, "Hey, what you did was okay." No, no, no. It's about acknowledging the messiness of human emotions and experiences. It's about taking a moment to understand that everyone is dealing with their own stuff. Empathy is your way of saying, "I see you, flaws and all. I may not agree with your actions, but I acknowledge that you're human, just like me."

Also, forgive yourself for harboring resentment, you too, are only human. Be kind to yourself; this journey takes time. Forgiveness is empowering and your way of taking control, breaking free from the shackles of past grievances. It's a symbol of empowerment. And crucially, it's a pivotal step in the emotional healing process. It creates space for self-love and acceptance, allowing your inner child to embark on a journey with a lighter heart and an open spirit. Practice empathy, not to let anyone off the hook, but to understand the depth and complexity of the human experience. It's a journey into compassion, a way of fostering connection and breaking down those walls that separate us. So, grab those metaphorical shoes, lace them up, and let's take a walk in someone else's world.

Amelia, 28, NYC

"Life in Manhattan mirrored my internal chaos, dragging the weight of resentment towards my estranged dad. His emotional absence left me feeling unworthy and utterly alone. One day, I'd had enough. The weight became too much to continue to carry so I decided to forgive – not for him, but for me.

It wasn't instant. I had to reflect on the roots of my resentment and think about painful memories I'd rather forget. Pouring those emotions onto paper, journaling became my main outlet for understanding what exactly I was feeling. Understanding my Dad's wounds without justifying his actions was a lot harder and a much longer process. For this, letter writing was my release. Even if I never gave him the letters, the weight slowly lifted, and life became more peaceful, way more joyful. Forgiveness made my heart lighter."

Derrick, 35, Ohio

"Forgiveness came when I realized how much the grudges I was carrying from childhood were still dragging me down – like a backpack full of stones from years of emotional neglect. I decided to forgive, not knowing it would be the key to getting my life back.

This definitely wasn't overnight. I had to accept my past for what it is and my parents for who they are. I'm still working on that part, but by realizing what I was lacking as a kid, I learned how to give those things to myself as an adult. I've forgiven them since. I know they did their best and now I can re-parent myself without all of the weight of grudges and resentment."

Transforming Negative Self-Talk

Ever notice that voice in your head? Yeah, the one that's not always the cheerleader you need. That negative self-talk is like an unwelcome guest crashing the party of your inner child. This harmful chatter often starts in those early years, echoing the critical tones of others. And guess what? Your sensitive inner child soaks it all in, leading to a cycle of emotional wounds impacting your self-esteem and overall well-being.

But don't worry – we're not here to stay stuck in that narrative. Let's shake things up and flip the script. Transforming that negative self-talk into positive affirmations is our game plan. First up, become buddies with awareness. Notice when those negative thoughts pop up, and don't stress – just observe. It's like catching that sneaky guest mid-sentence.

Once you start to notice those thoughts, we can now challenge and reframe them. Ask yourself, are they even legit? Or are they just echoes from the past? Now, let's create a list of personalized affirmations. Think of them as your inner child's hype squad – countering those negatives with positive, empowering vibes. You're turning the volume up on positivity and drowning out those old, negative tunes. And the trick? The more personal and tailored they are to your unique journey and dreams, the more effective they will be. It's like crafting a mantra that's all about you, resonating with your experiences and aspirations.

Need examples to kickstart your affirmation game? How about starting with affirmations focused on self-worth? Picture saying, "I am deserving of love and respect" – countering any lingering feelings of inadequacy. Or how about, "I am capable and competent" – a direct hit against self-doubt, reminding yourself of your strengths.

What about when you need a burst of resilience to overcome challenges? Try, "I embrace difficulties as opportunities for growth" – flipping the script on adversity and turning setbacks into stepping stones. And for a touch of joy and happiness, go for, "I am worthy of joy and happiness" – steering your inner child away from self-sacrifice and unworthiness.

These affirmations are like your personal power playlist. They're not just words; they're your daily dose of self-love and empowerment. So, go ahead, create your affirmations, let them be your inner child's anthem, and turn up the volume on positivity!

Repeat those affirmations regularly, especially in moments of doubt or stress. Also, don't be afraid to spice it up with visuals – vision boards or sticky notes in plain sight. Weave these affirmations into your daily routine. Morning rituals, journaling, bedtime reflections – whatever floats your boat. Consistent integration ensures that positive self-talk becomes second nature and tangible reminders make those affirmations even more potent!

Posted a new affirmation on your vision board? There's a high-five moment – celebrate your progress and acknowledge all victories, big or small! By embracing these strategies, you're not just flipping the script; you're giving your inner child a megaphone for self-love and growth. Positive affirmations? They're like the superhero cape for your inner dialogue. Let's get that dialogue centered on self-love, empowerment, and an unwavering belief in your worth.

Creating a Safe Inner Sanctuary

Inside the deepest, cozy corners of your thoughts lies a haven—a snug retreat where your inner child can kick back, feel secure, and flourish. Creating an inner sanctuary for interactions with your inner child to take place will allow for a comfortable place to be truly vulnerable.

Let's visualize a sanctuary together. First, make sure that you're in a comfy spot, take a deep breath, in for five seconds, and out for five seconds. We're dialing it down, the tension is releasing slowly from the top of your head and through your facial muscles. Your jaw loosens and your shoulders drop. Your body begins to settle, heavy into your position.

Now, close those eyes and envision a place that exudes safety, peace, and all-around warmth. It could be a beach, a forest glade, or the coziest room you can conjure. This is your unique sanctuary and should reflect what makes you feel secure. Trust those instincts, and let your imagination run wild.

Feel the imaginary sunlight on your skin, hear the soothing waves, and catch the scent of flowers in the breeze. Engage all your senses to make this mental retreat a vivid experience, like painting a masterpiece of comfort in your mind. Maybe there's a smell or a song from your youth that brings back joyful memories. All of these details add to the beautiful puzzle that will become your inner sanctuary.

As the final pieces of your safe space come together, imagine your inner child strolling in—a younger version of yourself, full of innocence and curiosity. Picture them with a big smile, ready and willing to share with you. Shower them with love, make them feel safe, and let them roam around this dreamy place and tweak it how they see fit. Ask them how they're doing, and what they need. And remind them that they are loved and appreciated.

The more you visit this space, the cozier and more inviting it will become. Practice this visualization regularly and when stress knocks, retreat to this mental haven. It's like building a bond with your inner child, creating a safe place for healing and self-discovery.

Guided Imagery Technique 1: Protective Bubble

Envision a protective bubble surrounding you and your inner child. This bubble is a shield against negativity. Picture it as a vibrant force field, keeping you both safe from any external stressors. Feel the warmth and security it provides.

Guided Imagery Technique 2: Guardian Figure

Imagine a guardian figure appearing in your sanctuary. It could be a wise mentor, a protective animal, or even a symbolic representation of strength. This figure watches over you and your inner child, offering guidance and support. Feel their reassuring presence.

Keep practicing these techniques. Your mental retreat is a powerful tool! Let's see how Emily and Michael faced their struggles before discovering the magic within their inner sanctuaries.

Emily, a resilient woman in her mid-30s, navigated the bustling streets of life, but beneath the surface, she carried the heavy remnants of a tumultuous past. Childhood experiences of emotional neglect had cast long shadows, leaving her grappling with feelings of unworthiness and insecurity. The echoes of those early years lingered, coloring her present with a constant undercurrent of chaos. It was in the midst of this emotional storm that Emily decided it was time for a change.

Seeking solace and healing, Emily embarked on a guided visualization journey. Her inner sanctuary became her refuge, strategically crafted to counterbalance the chaos that had defined her earlier years. The tranquil beach, a symbolic landscape of peace and renewal, was where the transformation unfolded. Closing her eyes to the imaginary sun warming her skin, Emily felt the rhythmic waves whispering promises of serenity. Along the shore, her inner child, timid and hesitant, emerged, mirroring the emotional state Emily had carried for far too long.

In the therapeutic act of building sandcastles, each grain of sand became a metaphor for the gradual release of Emily's emotional burdens. Through whispered conversations with her inner child, Emily compassionately acknowledged the pain they both had endured. The beach retreat wasn't just a picturesque scene; it became a tangible space where Emily cultivated healing. It became a sanctuary where she embraced the gentle process of reclaiming her inner self, gradually breaking free from the chains that bound her to a tumultuous past.

Now, let's shift our focus to Michael, a man in his early 40s, who grappled with the echoes of a tumultuous childhood marked by verbal criticism and unmet emotional needs. These experiences had planted seeds of self-doubt that flourished into adulthood, creating a dense emotional forest where shadows lurked at every turn. The echoes of criticism haunted his thoughts, casting doubts on his worthiness and capabilities. It was within this emotional forest that Michael sought refuge.

In his visualization, Michael chose a vast, sun-dappled forest as his inner sanctuary—a stark contrast to the shadows that had haunted him for years. The towering trees symbolized the formidable challenges he faced, challenges rooted in self-imposed limitations and the echoes of past criticisms. As he stepped into this inner sanctuary, Michael encountered his inner child—a younger self overshadowed by doubts and limitations. The therapeutic journey through the forest wasn't about escaping the shadows; it was about facing them head-on.

Nurturing his inner child amidst the greenery, Michael verbalized words of encouragement and empowerment. The forest, once harboring fears, transformed into a space for self-discovery and resilience. Each step became a conscious effort to unravel the intricate threads of his past, fostering self-compassion and empowerment. The forest, with its towering trees and dappled sunlight, became a backdrop for a transformative journey toward emotional well-being and self-discovery.

In these stories, the struggle was real, and the inner sanctuary wasn't just a picturesque escape; it was the canvas where these individuals painted the next chapters of their lives. The beach and the forest became the stages where healing unfolded, shadows were confronted, and the echoes of the past gradually dissipated, paving the way for emotional well-being and self-discovery.

Empowering Your Inner Child

♥

Recognizing Inner Strengths

Buckle up – this chapter is your personal guide to creating a cozy space where we'll explore recognition, set some boundaries, add a dash of playfulness, sprinkle some joy, and throw in a bit of celebration for your inner child's journey toward empowerment.

Let's kick it off by recognizing those inner strengths we both know are there. Imagine your inner child as your creativity maestro, bringing in fresh ideas and artistic vibes to spice up your daily life. That curiosity of yours? It's your guide to wonder, nudging you to explore new things and keep that childlike excitement alive.

Spontaneity is like your secret ingredient – that 'go with the flow' attitude injects joy and a willingness to dive into new experiences without overthinking. Resilience, embodied by your inner child, is your superhero power, bouncing back from setbacks with a positive vibe.

Authenticity is your sidekick, promoting genuine expression and a deeper understanding of your professional desires. Playfulness? It's the laughter in your work life, blending creativity with stress relief. Emotional intelligence takes the spotlight, helping you navigate complex emotions with grace and empathy.

Adaptability, a skill learned in childhood, becomes your professional ace, guiding you through career changes. Let's nurture a relationship with our inner child, letting these qualities shine for a more fulfilling and well-balanced journey. Who wouldn't want a sprinkle of that childhood magic every day, right?

With all of those strengths already inside of you, let's get personal and take a stroll down Memory Lane – remember those moments in childhood when you felt alive and free? What were you doing? How can you recreate that feeling now? What qualities are tied to your inner child? Which ones grew with you into adulthood?

Empowerment starts with acknowledgment. As you embrace the strengths of your inner child, a profound transformation unfolds. These qualities aren't just relics of a past self; they're the seeds of self-love for your present and future self. Recognizing the resilience, creativity, and authenticity within you is a catalyst for unleashing your full potential, paving the way for a journey where self-discovery and growth go hand in hand.

Setting Boundaries

Oh, the wonderful world of boundaries – you know, the little protective fence around the emotional playground of your inner child. These limits are all about preserving emotional safety, preventing overwhelm, and letting your true self shine without any fear. Think of them as filters, helping you keep that perfect balance in your life.

Healthy boundaries are a form of self-compassion, creating an environment where your inner child can flourish, heal, and just thrive. So, how do you set these magical limits? Well, it's not one-size-fits-all. Start by reflecting on your needs and values, understanding what vibes with you, and communicating it openly. Saying 'no' when needed is like a superhero move for self-care. It's not always the easiest thing to do, especially if you feel like you're letting someone down, but it's necessary. Listen to your gut – if something feels off, it's time to set a boundary. And hey, respect others' boundaries too, because it's a two-way street.

Let's bring in some scripts to make the boundary talk a breeze:

In the realm of work responsibilities, you might say something like, "I love the growth opportunities, but my plate's a bit full. Let's chat about tasks to keep things manageable so that I can provide the best quality." Or what about when it comes to personal time, try this on for size: "Starting next week, I'll need to carve out some time for myself. Evenings are my me-time. Let's plan our work stuff during office hours!"

Expressing emotional boundaries can be a bit more difficult, especially with those people in our lives who are a bit of emotional vampires. That being said, it could go like this: "I value our connection! Sometimes need space for my thoughts. Not about us, just to make sure I'm fully present when we're together." Or for social boundaries, you might share: "I love hanging out! Sometimes need recharge time though, hope you get it if I pass on plans. It's all about balance."

Clear communication is the key – be assertive, express your needs genuinely, and build relationships that respect everyone's well-being.

The Power of Play

It's playtime! This is the secret language your inner child speaks, bringing in all the good stuff like joy, creativity, and that sense of freedom we sometimes forget to cherish. Life gets pretty wild, right? And in the middle of all that chaos, play and leisure are the unsung heroes of your inner child. It's not just about reliving childhood games; it's a big deal for your well-being that often sneaks under the radar.

So, how do we tap into that carefree spirit? It's all about embracing playful activities – games, hobbies, creative endeavors, all letting our imaginations roam free. These moments of play aren't just a break; they're a magical portal back to the simple joys that lit up our childhood. Plus, they're a total game-changer for creativity, stress reduction, and that sense of wonder we sometimes misplace.

Incorporating play into our routines isn't just self-care; it's an investment in our mental and emotional well-being. It's like a celebration of life's lighter moments that keeps that inner child of yours alive, kicking, and thriving.

Remember those things you loved doing as a kid – drawing, playing an instrument, or crafting? Hobbies are like little joy factories. Saying 'yes' to unexpected adventures or activities that once made your smile breaks you away from routines – taking a spontaneous walk or trying a new restaurant can bring a burst of excitement.

What about turning exercise into a joyous adventure? Instead of dreading workouts, why not make them feel like playtime? Or nature!

It is the ultimate playground. A simple walk, a picnic in the park, or stargazing on a clear night – Whether it's dancing, hula hooping in the backyard, or joining a recreational sports league, these adventures let you experience the world as your canvas. Like letting the earth itself be your playmate.

Remember, the essence of play lies in the joy it brings. Find activities that resonate with you specifically, and allow yourself the freedom to play without judgment or expectation. An activity that makes you smile one day, may seem daunting the next. It's a wonderful exploration into your own joy and a way to keep the spirit of your inner child alive and thriving in your daily life.

Let me take you through two case studies that shout out the incredible magic of play in the lives of adults – meet Xenia and Victor, two everyday heroes who discovered rejuvenation through the sheer joy of incorporating play into their daily routines.

Case Study 1: Xenia's Journey to Rejuvenation Through Play

Background:

Xenia, a 35-year-old marketing executive, found herself caught in the demanding whirlwind of work and responsibilities. Burnout became a constant companion, affecting both her professional performance and personal life.

Intervention:

Recognizing the need for a change, Xenia decided to incorporate play into her routine. She started dedicating weekends to activities she enjoyed during her childhood – playing board games, exploring nature trails, and engaging in creative arts.

Results:

Over the course of a few months, Xenia experienced a remarkable rejuvenation. The playful activities served as a mental reset, allowing her to approach work with a refreshed perspective. The stress and tension that had accumulated gradually dissipated, and she found joy in the simplicity of playful moments. Not only did Xenia's creativity at work improve, but her overall well-being flourished, highlighting the rejuvenating effects of play for adults.

Case Study 2: Victor's Transformation Through Playful Exercise

Background:

Victor, a 42-year-old software developer, led a sedentary lifestyle that took a toll on both his physical health and mental well-being. The monotony of his routine left him feeling drained and uninspired.

Intervention:

Motivated to make a positive change, Victor decided to infuse play into his exercise routine. Instead of conventional workouts, he joined a recreational sports league. The focus shifted from regimented exercises to playing sports like soccer and basketball with a group of like-minded adults.

Results:

The impact was transformative. Not only did Victor witness a significant improvement in his physical health, but the playful nature of the sports brought a sense of joy back into his life. The camaraderie with teammates added a social element, combating feelings of isolation. Victor's overall energy levels soared, and he discovered that play could be a powerful catalyst for physical and mental rejuvenation. The experience highlighted the profound effects of incorporating playful activities into adult lifestyles for holistic well-being.

In essence, these case studies exemplify that play is not just a childhood indulgence but a potent source of rejuvenation, capable of fostering creativity, alleviating stress, and bringing about holistic well-being in the lives of adults like Xenia and Victor.

Cultivating Joy and Wonder

Amidst the whirlwind of life, I urge you to take a moment to reconnect with those sources of joy and wonder that might be quietly waiting in the wings. Embrace that childlike curiosity within you, the spark that's eager to explore activities bringing genuine delight. Whether you're diving into playful pursuits, revisiting childhood hobbies, or simply soaking in the beauty around you, gift yourself these moments of joy. In these moments, you'll not only find respite from life's pressures but also a revitalizing force that breathes new life into your days.

Consider, for instance, the ease of mindful playtime. Imagine setting aside dedicated moments where the only goal is to engage in activities that bring you joy. It could be drawing, building with blocks, or simply experimenting with different art forms. Envision yourself dancing like nobody's watching, whether it's in the privacy of your home or during a lively dance class. The rhythmic movement becomes a joyful expression, creating a deep connection between the music and your own body.

Or, imagine a practice that allows you to cultivate a sense of presence and wonder in everyday moments. Imagine focusing on your breath, observing sensations in your body, and appreciating the simplicity of the present. Picture mindfulness grounding you, inviting joy into the now. Practice looking in the mirror and appreciating how much you've grown and how beautiful you are in the present moment.

Remember, the key is to approach these activities with openness and curiosity. Allow joy and wonder to naturally unfold in your life. After all, there is an abundance all around you just waiting to be noticed.

I want to share a couple of personal stories that were sent in about two amazing individuals who rediscovered joy and transformed their lives through inner child work, specifically by rediscovery the power of play and small joys.

Meet Alban, a 40-year-old professional caught up in the relentless pace of corporate life. He was feeling the weight of responsibilities, and it was taking a serious toll on his well-being. Alban decided to make a change and dove into inner child work. Through guided exercises and reflection, he revisited memories from his carefree childhood days.

During this journey, Alban found profound joy in simple, childlike activities. Blowing bubbles became a therapeutic release. He started expressing creativity through drawing with vibrant markers which allowed him to tap into his playful side. Even the act of skipping, something he hadn't done in years, became a simple gateway to rekindling the sense of wonder and joy buried beneath the daily grind. Committing to inner child work wasn't just about unlocking his youthful spirit; it became a daily practice that guided him toward a more balanced and fulfilling existence.

Now, let's talk about Elaine, a 35-year-old facing past traumas and emotional challenges. She embarked on a transformative journey of inner child healing as a crucial part of her therapeutic process. Elaine bravely delved into the recesses of childhood memories, addressing long-suppressed emotions with compassion and understanding.

In the course of this inner exploration, Elaine made a delightful discovery – reconnecting with the playful and innocent qualities of her younger self became an unexpected wellspring of joy. Engaging in activities that mirrored the carefree spirit of her childhood, such as swinging at the park, molding creations with clay, and hosting movie nights with her friends featuring her favorite childhood films, turned out to be therapeutic sources of genuine happiness. Through the transformative power of inner child work, Elaine not only found profound healing but also rekindled a sense of joy that seamlessly integrated into her ongoing journey of emotional well-being.

These stories show how rediscovering joy can be a powerful journey of healing and transformation. Life has its challenges, but it's incredible to witness the resilience and joy that can emerge when we reconnect with our inner child.

Celebrating Small Victories

It's time to celebrate you! Those little wins that might seem insignificant throughout the day, week, or year, can actually truly brighten your path and boost your motivation in the long-run.

Why are these victories a big deal? Well, they're like little milestones, marking your progress and resilience. Recognizing them is like giving yourself a pat on the back, especially in the face of life's challenges.

Celebratory rituals are your personal ways of saying, "Hey, I did it!" One idea, that is a personal favorite, is to throw a dance party. I'm not saying to go out and invite the entire neighborhood into your home.

We're talking about cranking up your favorite song and dancing like nobody's watching; if that's in your underwear, a ballgown, or nothing at all so be it. The joy and freedom of movement is a celebration in itself.

Another option is to treat yourself – whether it's a scoop of your favorite ice cream, a piece of expensive chocolate, or that sweater you've been eyeing in the window for months, indulge a bit. You've earned it. As you're celebrating the wins in life, don't forget to document them. Create a journal or creative project by documenting all of your victories in a special place. Pour out your thoughts and emotions, savoring the feeling of accomplishment – it's like creating a personalized trophy cabinet of your wins – a tangible reminder of your capabilities. Remember, celebrating small victories is a personal journey, so feel free to mix and match ideas or come up with your very own. The key is to make it enjoyable and meaningful for you!

Let's get into two stories that show the incredible power of celebrating the little victories in life.

Meet Joanne, a vibrant 24-year-old facing the challenges of adulthood. Tired of self-doubt, Joanne decided to flip the script by embracing the magic of celebrating small wins. She kicked things off by starting a victory journal – a personal record of every win, big or small. Whether it was finishing tasks at work, conquering fears, or making moves on passion projects, Joanne made sure to celebrate absolutely everything. Plus, she added a weekly ritual of treating herself, like indulging in a favorite dessert or buying herself something special. Those small celebrations? They became Joanne's secret for growing confidence, laying the foundation for a life filled with self-belief and purpose.

Now, she celebrates all of the wins without thinking twice about it and has cultivated a truly meaningful relationship with her inner child.

Now, let's go to Mathias, a 37-year-old at a life crossroads, hungry for a change. Seeking transformation, he started embracing the art of celebrating the little things. Daily goals became his thing – from tackling chores to dedicating time to beloved hobbies. He started every morning by making a list of his goals for the day. Every achievement, no matter how small, got a moment of heartfelt acknowledgment and celebration. Mathias even created an "Achievement Wall" at home, to visually celebrate his progress. This wall turned into his go-to motivation during tough times. With each small win, Mathias felt a surge of confidence taking charge of his life. Those victories became stepping stones, pushing him towards bigger and bigger achievements and reigniting his pursuit of long-held dreams. Mathias's story? It's a reminder that celebrating the small stuff isn't just a thing – it's a powerful force that can rewrite your story and set you on a path of personal empowerment.

So, as you dive into the journey of rediscovering and empowering your inner child, let Joanne and Mathias be your buddies. Let them inspire you to notice and cheer for those small victories. May this become your daily ritual, guiding you to a life overflowing with joy, purpose, and a whole lot of self-love.

Overcoming Inner Child Challenges

♥

Facing Fears and Insecurities

Let's talk about something we've all carried with us since childhood –
those fears and insecurities that find a way into our adult lives. You
know, the ones that play hide and seek with our emotions. So, buckle
up because we're going to get into the nitty-gritty of it all.

Ever heard of the fear of abandonment? It's like this deep-seeded worry
about being left alone or unloved, usually rooted in early experiences
of neglect or loss. Imagine feeling clingy in relationships or constantly
needing reassurance – that's the abandonment fear playing its tune.

What about rejection sensitivity? A constant, penetrating fear of not
being 'good enough' or being hypersensitive to criticism. It's like having an emotional radar that's always on high alert for potential rejec-

tion. It's tough, right? This fear can make forming and maintaining relationships feel like navigating a tricky maze full of thorns that you can't seem to avoid.

Low self-esteem is another player in this chaotic emotional orchestra. Imagine negative feedback or unrealistic expectations during childhood creating feelings of inadequacy and low self-worth. Adults with low self-esteem might find themselves fishing for external validation to make up for what they think are shortcomings.

Trust issues, anyone? If betrayal or broken trust marked your childhood, you might find it tricky to open up to others as an adult. Vulnerability becomes a really scary prospect, with an inner child that's on high alert for any potential harm or abandonment.

Fear of failure, oh boy. It's worrying about making mistakes, usually fueled by high expectations or harsh criticism during childhood. The inner child might resist taking risks or pursuing goals, fearing rejection or disapproval.

Perfectionism takes the stage too. Imagine having this relentless pursuit of perfection, born from childhood experiences where achievements were tightly linked to self-worth. It's like setting standards that will never be attainable, leading to stress and burnout.

Insecurity in relationships is no stranger either. Unresolved childhood attachment issues can rear their head as adult insecurities – fear of intimacy, communication struggles, or patterns of clinginess or avoidance. And this tends to go hand in hand with the fear of vulnerability. The fear of opening up emotionally is often stemming from childhood experiences where expressing feelings was discouraged or met with criticism. Adults with this fear might find it hard to share their emotions openly.

Whew! That was a lot, right? But here's the best part – facing and overcoming these fears involves a mix of self-awareness, self-compassion, and some therapeutic techniques that are all right at your fingertips.

The inner child work that you're in the midst of is a magical journey where visualization, conscious self-love, and realizing mistakes are a blessing all become your savior. Guided imagery helps you connect with your younger self, leaving space for you to nurture that inner child with love and compassion. Letter writing is another move – heartfelt words to your inner child, expressing understanding and reassurance from your wiser adult self. It's a dialogue that bridges the past and present, paving the way for healing and guidance.

Mindful awareness and conversations with your inner self let you observe and acknowledge fears without judgment, creating a non-reactive and accepting stance towards distressing thoughts. Positive affirmations become your daily cheerleaders, replacing negative self-talk with words that lift you up. Celebrating achievements, no matter how tiny, is like throwing a party for yourself. It's all about acknowledging progress and focusing on your strengths. Your success journal? It's your tangible record of growth, a reminder to embrace your journey.

Remember, progress might be slow and steady but your inner child is cheering you on!

In the tapestry of personal growth, the extraordinary stories of Lisa and Benny stand as vivid threads, weaving resilience and courage into the very fabric of the human spirit. As we get into their inspiring tales, we witness the transformative power that lies in confronting and triumphing over inner child challenges.

Lisa, a courageous journey of self-discovery that unfolded against the backdrop of a challenging childhood marked by emotional neglect. Lisa carried the weight of unworthiness into adulthood, a heavy burden that held her back from her true potential. Yet, like the protagonist of her own story, Lisa refused to be defined by her past. She embarked on a quest for healing, seeking the guidance of inner child work to unravel the complexities of her internal challenges. Guided visualizations and emotional explorations became her tools of empowerment, allowing her to confront the wounds of her past with resilience and compassion. Lisa didn't stop there; she started writing letters to her younger self, offering words of comfort and understanding. With each step, she embraced her vulnerabilities, revealing an inner strength she never knew existed. As the chapters unfolded, Lisa's narrative underwent a profound transformation, ultimately leading to the embrace of self-love and a newfound sense of worthiness. Her journey serves as an inspiring testament to the transformative power of courage and the commitment to self-discovery.

Now, let's turn the pages to Benny – a triumph over adversity and addiction. Benny's early years were marred by adversity, setting the stage for a formidable battle with addiction in his adult life. But Benny, resilient, chose the path of courage. Seeking professional help, he enrolled in a rehabilitation program that integrated therapeutic approaches like inner child work and mindfulness. Benny's journey of self-discovery and healing was no easy feat; it required intense self-reflection and a brave confrontation with the pain rooted in his inner child. Group therapy sessions became spaces of vulnerability, connection, and support. Overcoming addiction wasn't just about breaking free from substances for Benny – it was a profound journey of reclaiming his authentic self.

Lisa and Benny's stories beckon us to confront our inner child challenges with the same courage and determination, knowing that healing is not just a destination but a transformative adventure waiting to unfold in the pages of our lives.

Dealing with Inner Criticism

Now let's unravel the art of silencing that pesky inner critic and fostering a more compassionate relationship with ourselves. Imagine this as a friendly chat where we're exploring ways to revolutionize the way we talk to ourselves.

At the very start, it's essential to take a moment and shine a light on that pesky little inner critic. It's unraveling the tangled knot of negative self-talk. As soon as the inner critic kicks off its verbal assault, our first line of defense is awareness. You become vigilant an observer, catching those critical thoughts in action. You notice when the inner critic begins its familiar tirade, pointing out mistakes or amplifying self-doubt.

But we're not going to stop there; you're not merely bystanders to our own mental chatter. You will become an active questioner. Interrogate those negative thoughts, demanding evidence for their validity. Challenge the inner critic's assumptions and consider alternative perspectives. It's a process of turning the spotlight onto the accuracy of these critical remarks, dissecting them to reveal the often unfounded nature of their claims.

This isn't about passive acceptance; it's a courageous act of questioning the credibility of our inner critic. Just because a thought surfaces doesn't make it true, and by probing these assumptions, you can reclaim a sense of control over your internal narrative. It's a step towards building resilience against the undermining influence of the inner critic, paving the way for a more self-compassionate and empowering mindset. So, here's to the detective work of recognizing, questioning, and challenging that inner critic.

Self-compassion is the real superpower here, though. Imagine treating yourself with the same kindness you'd offer a friend on a bad day. It's about time to become our own best friend, right?

By demonstrating mindfulness, we're actually observing the inner critic without getting all tangled up. Once you become aware of this critic, can sit back and listen, you can combat it with positive affirmations. When the inner critic goes on a rampage, counteract it with empowering phrases. "I'm doing the best I can," or "Everyone makes mistakes." It's a game-changer.

Turning self-criticism into self-compassion is a transformative journey. And embracing the imperfection of it all allows you to view setbacks as stepping stones for growth, rather than reasons to throw a pity party. As Elizabeth Gilbert puts it, "Embrace the glorious mess that you are."

Managing Overwhelm and Stress

Navigating the whirlwind of the world can stir up echoes of childhood stress. But fear not, there are strategies that we'll get into together that will support your inner child during overwhelming moments and create a sanctuary of calm within the chaos.

For starters, breathing exercises are like hitting the reset button for your nervous system – inhale slowly, exhale mindfully, and find pockets of stillness. It's a simple yet effective way to bring that inner peace. This exercise has a way of grounding you in mindfulness inviting you to engage all of your senses – touch, sight, smell, and sound – giving your inner child a front-row seat to the present moment right alongside you. This sensory awareness becomes your anchor, dialing down overwhelm as you embrace the here and now.

When breathing and being mindful just won't cut it and the stress is real, consider a creative endeavor or a comfort object. It could be art, writing, playing your favorite album, or whatever else makes your heart sing. These expressions are like therapy sessions for your inner child. They let out the stress and give your inner kiddo a sense of control. Also, don't be fooled, comfort objects aren't just for kids. An old, comfy blanket or a favorite stuffed animal can honestly be like a security blanket for the little you inside.

By weaving these stress-busting techniques into your routine, you're not just managing stress and overwhelm; you're creating a haven for your inner child. It's a game-changer for resilience, emotional well-being, and finding that soothing anchor when life gets to be a bit too much. We've found that discovering pockets of calm in the day-to-day serves as invaluable anchors. Here are three personal anecdotes that attest to the transformative power of discovering serenity amidst chaos.

The Coffee Shop Serenity

"Buckle up for my Monday morning saga. So, there I am, drowning in deadlines and an inbox that won't stop dinging. Stress levels through the roof. What's my genius move? I declare a timeout. It was all that

I could think to do. So I got up, left the building, and strolled over to the nearby coffee shop, got my trusty latte, and claimed a cozy corner. In the middle of the hustle and bustle, with the coffee scent doing its thing and the low hum of chatter, guess what? It turned into an unexpected sanctuary. Sipped that latte like I was sipping life, and voila! Life's full of surprises, my friend. "

Nature's Reset Button

"So, there I was, right in the middle of this crazy week – work was getting too overwhelming, and life's just stressing me. Total chaos! So I got up and decided to just go outside and take a walk. I left my phone and yeah, that happened. I found myself surrounded by these massive trees and leaves doing a little dance for me. And before I knew it, the stress had dissipated. Poof, gone. Nature's magic reset button, I tell you. Lesson learned: when life's throwing a fit, nature's got this amazing way of bringing the calm back. Who knew, right? "

Healing from Disappointment

Dealing with disappointment can feel like having a heart-to-heart with your inner child. It's one of those things we all go through. So, let those emotions flow – it's all part of the game. Talk to your inner kiddo like you would with a friend, letting them know it's totally okay to feel the way they do. And think of setbacks as plot twists in the epic story of your life, not as epic fails. Remind your inner child that mistakes are just life's way of keeping things interesting.

Let me share some moves that will amp up the good vibes. Picture a safe space where your inner child can spill all the tea, scribble feelings, and uncover some real-life lessons. Consider jotting it down. We know we're all forgetful and trust me, these are lessons you won't want to forget. It's like creating a story of personal growth, documented and legit. Add in some super personal affirmations that are like love notes for your inner child, reminding them they're worthy of love and understanding even when things go south. It's all about building that self-worth and acceptance.

Sometimes, we get so caught up in the big battles that we forget the little victories can mean it all. Celebrate those moments like your inner child just won a gold medal – whether it's nailing a presentation, conquering a fear, or just getting out of bed on a tough day. These victories may seem small, but they're the glue that holds the big picture together. It's like building a fortress of resilience brick by brick. So, grab that imaginary trophy, throw some confetti in your mind, and let your inner child revel in the glory of those tiny, magnificent wins.

Disappointment, a universal facet of the human experience, often resonates deeply with the inner child. By approaching it through the lens of the inner child and incorporating these exercises, you can foster a compassionate and growth-oriented perspective, turning setbacks into opportunities for personal development and resilience.

Let's dive into some motivational stories of resilience, where individuals transformed disappointment into stepping stones for personal and emotional growth. Witness how these experiences became catalysts for profound healing.

From Setback to Triumph:

Maya, a young professional, faced a major setback when she didn't secure the job she had dreamed of for years. Disappointment and self-doubt loomed large, but Maya chose resilience over despair. Instead of viewing it as a failure, she reframed it as an opportunity to reassess her goals. Embracing the setback as a chance for personal growth, Maya sought new experiences and skill development. She engaged in networking, pursued additional certifications, and explored different industries. Eventually, Maya landed a role that not only aligned with her skills but also brought unexpected fulfillment. The disappointment became a catalyst for a more resilient and adaptable version of herself, emphasizing that setbacks can be stepping stones to uncharted and rewarding territories.

Turning Adversity into Strength:

Arthur faced a life-altering disappointment when a long-term relationship ended unexpectedly. Initially shattered, Arthur chose not to let this setback define their narrative. Instead, he embarked on a transformative journey of self-discovery and emotional healing. Arthur sought therapy to navigate the complexities of emotions and learned to embrace vulnerability as a source of strength. Through self-reflection and support from loved ones, Arthur gradually reconstructed a sense of identity and purpose. The disappointment, once a profound wound, became a catalyst for resilience. Arthur emerged from the experience stronger, more self-aware, and equipped with the emotional tools to navigate future challenges. The journey highlighted that even the most profound disappointments can be transformative stepping stones toward greater emotional growth and resilience.

Navigating Relationships

Exploring the world of the inner child is like turning on a light in the basement of our relationships. It's where all the emotional blueprints from our childhood hang out. Imagine this little version of you, just a ball of feelings and impressions, essentially running the show in your adult connections. So, if you were all about attention or validation back then, surprise – those are still on the wishlist in your grown-up relationships. It's like our younger selves have this subtle but prominent influence on how we connect, express needs, and handle challenges today.

Think of it as the script behind your relationship dialogue. If expressing emotions got tricky in the past, your inner child might still be a bit shy about opening up. That might translate into holding back or taking a step back when things get intense. Unraveling these inner child threads is like saying, "Hey, let's understand why we do what we do in relationships." It's about making room for both you and your partner to connect authentically, knowing that those little versions of yourselves are part of the story.

In the world of nurturing healthy emotional connections, treating your inner child with a bit of tenderness goes a long way. Start with honest communication – create a space where you can spill your feelings, needs, and fears without feeling like you're stepping on landmines. It builds trust and intimacy, making your inner child feel seen and heard. And of course, we can't forget about the fine art of active listening. Tune in to your partner's emotions without slapping labels on them. It's a bridge between your past emotional blueprints and the present lovefest, deepening your understanding of each other's inner landscapes.

When the going gets tough, treat yourself with kindness. Recognize that hiccups are just growth opportunities, not reasons to whip out the self-blame stick. By giving your inner child a dose of this compassion, you're setting the stage for emotional resilience. Oh, and boundaries – they're just necessary in relationships. Acknowledge that both of you bring your own emotional history to the table. Respect that, and you create a haven where both your inner kids can flourish. It's a mix of empathy, self-compassion, and a commitment to nurturing a space for both your inner child and your partner.

So how do you find that sweet spot between being your own person and creating a strong, intertwined bond in a relationship?

Imagine this: personal hobbies. It's a playground for individuality. You get the freedom to dive into your unique interests, be it painting, playing an instrument, a sport... whatever! It's all about expressing that beautiful individuality. Now, throw in a twist – couples can support each other's passions. Attend events together, cheer each other on, or simply give space for those solo pursuits. It's the dance of individuality and partnership, all in one.

Now, communication – the heartbeat of any connection. Being authentically you means open and honest talks. Share your thoughts, dreams, and all those feelings without holding back. But here's the magic: in a healthy partnership, there's this understanding and active listening that should naturally happen. Partners become the biggest cheerleaders for each other's goals, offering emotional high-fives and celebrating all the personal victories. It's about sharing the real stuff.

Boundaries! Set those personal limits for self-care and keep your own space sacred. Maybe it's some alone time, respecting preferences, or laying out specific needs. Now, here's the beauty: in an interdependent dance, partners honor each other's boundaries. That personal space can be like oxygen – essential. By backing these limits, couples groove together in harmony.

These are a snapshot of how individuals can show off their uniqueness while building a cozy, connected relationship. Balancing both sides brings richness and resilience to the partnership. It's like creating a masterpiece where individual strokes blend into a beautiful, shared canvas.

The Inner Child and Relationships

♥

Attracting Healthy Relationships

Embarking on the journey of healing your inner child is like unlocking the door to a whole new world, especially for healthier relationships. Delving into the layers of your past experiences with a knowledgeable and compassionate lens is all about understanding the roots of your behaviors and reactions. This newfound self-awareness? It will be your guiding light, helping you navigate present challenges with emotional regulation and resilience.

The magic? This process nudges you to embrace your vulnerabilities, paving the way for a deeper connection not just with yourself but also with the inner child dynamics of your partner. Healing your inner child means breaking free from those destructive relationship patterns, building secure attachments, and nurturing open communication. It's a compassionate journey of reparenting yourself, and cultivating a profound sense of self-love and understanding.

And the ripple effects extend into your relationships, creating a space filled with authenticity, empathy, and genuine connections – the real foundation of healthier and more fulfilling bonds.

Now, let's talk about how to foster connections that honor the inner child. It's a tender and intentional endeavor, rooted in knowledge, empathy, and compassion. Start by understanding your inner child dynamics through introspection. Acknowledge those vulnerabilities and needs from childhood, treating them with the tenderness you'd offer to a younger you. And in relationships, extend this understanding to your partner, creating a space where both inner children feel seen and valued. It can be an incredibly powerful thing to simply remember that your partner was once a little child who may not have always been taken care of properly.

Open communication is the key. Share your insights and actively listen to your partner's experiences, creating a mutual exchange of vulnerability. When emotions are on the table, practice empathy. Understand that reactions might be rooted in past wounds. During conflicts, approach with patience and a genuine desire to understand, leaving judgment and criticism at the door.

Bringing in the joy and playfulness of the inner child can make this process easier and way more fun. Create rituals of connection – shared hobbies, playful activities, or simply spending quality time together. Celebrate each other's successes, big or small, providing the support and encouragement needed for continued growth. It's like sprinkling a bit of magic into your relationships, making them truly authentic and fulfilling.

As you navigate the intricacies of your partner's inner child, remember that healing is an ongoing process. Be a source of reassurance and comfort, offering a haven where vulnerabilities can be expressed without fear of judgment. Establish and respect boundaries, recognizing that each person's inner child deserves protection and acknowledgment. By fostering connections that honor the inner child, you not only deepen the bond with your partner but also create a nurturing space where both individuals can continue to heal, grow, and thrive in the warmth of compassionate connection.

Clara's Journey to Love:

Clara, after embarking on a profound journey of healing her inner child, discovered a newfound sense of self-love and resilience. Having navigated the complexities of past wounds and insecurities, she entered a period of self-discovery and growth. In this transformative process, Clara learned to embrace vulnerability and communicate openly about her needs and fears. As she ventured into the dating world post-healing, Clara approached relationships with a deep understanding of herself and an empathetic lens toward potential partners. This newfound authenticity attracted James, a kindred spirit who had also traversed his healing journey. Their connection was rooted in shared vulnerability, mutual support, and a commitment to understanding each other's inner child dynamics. Clara and James found fulfillment in a relationship where healing wasn't just an individual endeavor but a shared journey, creating a space where their inner children thrived in the warmth of mutual love and understanding.

Miguel's Path to Partnership:

Miguel's journey of healing his inner child led to a profound transformation in his approach to relationships. Having grappled with trust issues and fear of vulnerability, Miguel undertook the challenging but rewarding process of self-discovery and healing. As he emerged with a newfound sense of self-worth and emotional resilience, Miguel crossed paths with Lila. Their connection was built on a foundation of mutual growth and understanding. Lila, too, had undergone her own healing journey, and their shared experiences created a unique bond. Together, they navigated the intricacies of their inner child dynamics with patience and empathy. Their relationship became a sanctuary where both Miguel and Lila felt seen, heard, and valued. Post-healing, Miguel found not only a life partner but a companion in growth—a relationship that honored their individual journeys while celebrating the shared joy of building a fulfilling and nurturing partnership.

Communicating Needs and Desires

Effective communication is a dance where empathy must take the lead. To master this art, start by acknowledging your inner child's needs and expressing your feelings authentically. Instead of just stating concerns, share how situations make you feel, allowing your partner to connect with the underlying emotions. By infusing humor and playfulness into conversations to create a lighthearted atmosphere honoring the joyous spirit of the inner child, you'll be able to create a shared emotional dialogue, where both partners feel heard, understood, and cherished.

Expressing Vulnerability:

Imagine you and your partner are catching up, and you feel the need to share what's been on your mind. You might say, "Hey, I've been feeling a bit overwhelmed lately. It takes me back to when I was a kid, and things felt uncertain. I need some extra love and support right now." Your partner responds with a supportive, "Of course, I'm here for you. What's been on your mind?" Now, pretend you're in this scenario with your partner, taking turns expressing vulnerability and offering support.

Active Listening and Validation:

In a conversation about your partner's challenging day, they shared, "Today was tough. I felt like nothing was going right." Your response is empathetic, "I'm here for you. It sounds like it was really challenging. Can you share more about what happened?" To practice active listening and validation, switch roles with your partner. Experience expressing and receiving support in a role-play scenario.

Conflict Resolution:

Picture navigating a disagreement with your partner. You bring up the issue, saying, "I noticed we had different perspectives on [the issue]. It brought up some old feelings for me, and I want to make sure we understand each other." Your partner responds with understanding, "I didn't realize it was affecting you that way. Let's talk it through and find a resolution that works for both of us." Now, simulate a disagreement in a role-play scenario, focusing on expressing feelings, understanding each other, and finding a resolution.

Playful Communication:

Think about infusing playfulness into any conversation with your partner. You suggest, "I was thinking, wouldn't it be fun to plan a little spontaneous adventure this weekend? Something to bring out our inner kids!" Your partner responds excitedly, "That sounds like a blast! What do you have in mind?" Experiment with incorporating playfulness into discussions in a role-play scenario, allowing for a lighter and more enjoyable exchange.

These scripts and role-play scenarios are like your own personal communication toolkit. Feel free to tweak them to match your vibe and comfort levels in your relationship.

Now, let's get into some real stories from people who've seen their relationships do a 180, all thanks to clear and empathetic communication.

Wilber, 34, Colorado: "Communication totally flipped our relationship on its head, in a good way. We used to tap dance around problems, but now, armed with effective communication tricks, we just lay it all out there. It's like we've got a roadmap for emotions, and our connection has hit a whole new level."

Jason, 28, California: "Communication used to be our Achilles' heel, but once we brought in active listening and vulnerability-sharing, things got seriously good. Validating each other's feelings turned our talks into a safe space. Conflicts are now chances to understand, and our bond is rock solid."

Mia, 42, New York: "After years of crossed wires, we decided to fine-tune our communication. Expressing needs and listening without judgment? Total game-changer. It's not just talking; it's hearing each other. Our relationship is now this space where we feel truly seen and understood."

Blake and Dakota, 30 and 28, Texas: "As a couple, we used to go to war over everything! Stuff that didn't even matter. But once we realized our communication was on shaky ground and did something about it, everything shifted. Now we've got the tools to support and love each other the way we deserve."

Maria, 36, in Florida, found joy again through playful communication: "Injecting humor into serious talks was a game-changer. It's crazy how a bit of laughter can dissolve tension. Clear communication not only leveled up our relationship but made us feel more connected and resilient."

The Role of Intimacy and Vulnerability

The nitty-gritty of relationships—intimacy and vulnerability. They're weaving this magical thread of connection that goes way beyond just having a friend. Intimacy is this beautiful art of peeling back the layers, showing off the real, unfiltered you. It's a dance where you and your partner waltz through emotions, and spill dreams, fears, and desires. This openness creates this sacred bubble where both of you feel truly seen, heard, and loved for exactly who you are. Intimacy? It's that magic that builds a deep connection, a bridge between your hearts that goes way beneath the surface, embracing all the beauty in your imperfections and vulnerabilities.

Now, vulnerability—it's this brave move of baring your soul, giving your partner a backstage pass to your thoughts and emotions. It's not a weakness thing; it's a powerhouse move of strength and trust. When we let ourselves be vulnerable, we're saying, "Hey, I get it. Life's a rollercoaster of joy, pain, and growth." This mutual vulnerability becomes the rock-solid base for genuine connection. Partners support each other through the ups and downs of life. It's this beautiful dance of intimacy and vulnerability that turns relationships into havens of understanding, compassion, and unwavering support—a shared journey where the warmth of real connection blooms.

Here's your roadmap to navigate this courageous journey:

1. Feel Those Feels: Start by checking in with yourself. What's going on in your emotional world? Reflect on your feelings and why they're there. This self-awareness is your ticket to authentic expression.

2. Timing is Everything: Find a cozy, distraction-free spot to chat with your partner. Timing matters, so choose a moment when you both can focus without the rush.

3. "I" Before "You": Use "I" statements to share your feelings without pointing fingers. Instead of saying, "You always make me feel..." go for "I feel overwhelmed when...". This will let your partner know that you're taking accountability for your feelings and allow them the space to respond without feeling critiqued or attacked.

4. Details, Please: Get specific about your emotions. Share details about the situation or behavior triggering your feelings. It paints a clearer picture for your partner.

5. Express Your Needs: Vulnerability often comes with needs. Whether it's support, understanding, or a change, communicate what would make you feel more supported.

6. Listen Up: Be an active listener. When your partner shares, listen with full attention, validate their feelings, and respond with empathy. It sets the stage for open communication.

7. Read Between the Lines: Vulnerability isn't just about words. Pay attention to non-verbal cues—body language and facial expressions. Sometimes, they speak louder than words.

8. Be Patient: Your partner might need time to process. Be patient and ditch the expectation of instant solutions. The goal is understanding and connection, not quick fixes.

9. No Judgment Zone: Create a space where both of you feel safe being vulnerable. Mutual understanding and acceptance lay the groundwork for a strong, nurturing relationship.

10. Therapy's a Team Player: If vulnerability feels like a tough game, consider bringing in a pro—therapists or counselors can offer a neutral space and tools to ace these conversations.

Remember, vulnerability is a two-way street in a healthy relationship. With these steps, you're building a foundation for open communication and strengthening that emotional bond with your partner. You got this!

Let me spill the tea on some heartwarming stories that'll make you feel all warm and fuzzy!

Tom and Jessica's Late-Night Heart-to-Heart:

Picture this – Tom and Jessica, both in their early thirties, decided to dive deep into the juicy stuff – their dreams and fears. Tom spilled the beans about wanting a career change, throwing in all his uncertainties and fears about it. Jessica, being the awesome partner she is, spilled the tea about her lifelong dream of kickstarting a business. Can you believe it? In this total vulnerability fest, they uncovered a shared fear of biting the dust and this crazy mutual desire to cheer each other on. Suddenly, they realized they weren't just ride-or-die partners; they were the dynamic duo conquering the dream world together.

Miles and Emily's Retro Wounds Cleanup:

Now, let's talk about Miles and Emily, the OG couple married for over a decade. They were like, "You know what? Time to deal with those old wounds!" Miles got real about how his childhood left some dents on his self-esteem. Meanwhile, Emily spilled the beans about the emotional baggage from an ex that just wouldn't leave her alone. But guess what? Their vulnerability party became a healing hotspot. They held each other tight, helped each other patch up those old wounds, and bam – their connection got stronger than ever. Sharing those deep fears not only brought them comfort but also a truckload of acceptance and love. The journey of healing together turned their relationship into this rock-solid bond that could weather any storm. Talk about a power couple!

Inner Child Influence on Parenting

This wild ride called parenting together, where our own little kiddo selves are doing some serious cha-cha in the background. Our own childhood memories, the good, the bad, and the ugly, shape the way we raise our own tiny humans. It's like a dance between the past and the present, and our inner child is the star of the show, pulling strings in our parenting playbook.

Ever notice how your inner child whispers in your ear when you're parenting? Maybe it's the need for validation or the ghost of neglect creeping in. But here's the deal: recognizing these patterns gives us the power to consciously choose how we respond to our kiddos. It's like a superhero move, breaking free from old cycles and creating a space where our little ones can grow and thrive.

Embracing our inner child is like tapping into a superpower. It lets us connect with our kiddos on a whole new level—bringing in the joy, curiosity, and creativity that make childhood awesome. But, it also means being mindful of those sneaky triggers and old wounds that may pop up. Knowing them is like having a compass, guiding us away from generational patterns and toward a nurturing environment.

Now, here's where the rubber meets the road. Breaking those generational cycles and becoming a conscious parent is a journey, my friend. Start by taking a peek into your inner child world. Reflect on what shaped your upbringing, the good stuff, and the not-so-great stuff. This self-awareness is your secret sauce, helping you choose the kind of parent you want to be.

When you're in the parenting trenches, stay present in the moment. Tune in to your kiddo's needs, emotions, and unique personality. Let your inner child's playful spirit join the party, making the journey a harmonious space for growth. And when challenges hit, take a deep breath. Your reactions might be influenced by your own past, but that pause gives you the power to respond consciously, breaking free from those old patterns.

Keep those lines of communication wide open. Create a safe space for your kiddo to express themselves, share stories from your own childhood, and be a model of resilience. Unconditional love is your magic wand, creating a nurturing environment where your child feels cherished for being their authentic selves.

Remember, you're not alone in this. Seek support from parenting communities, books, or pros. Breaking generational cycles is a team effort, and surrounding yourself with resources strengthens your super-parent powers. The journey of conscious parenting isn't about being perfect—it's about growing and learning every day. So, go ahead, embrace that inner child with kindness, choose mindful responses, and let's pave the way for a new story—a legacy of love, understanding, and being fully present with our little rockstars.

Peggy's Journey to Conscious Parenting

Peggy, a mother of two in her early thirties, embarked on a transformative journey of conscious parenting by delving into the echoes of her own inner child. Raised in an environment where emotional expression was stifled, Peggy recognized the need for change in her parenting approach. She began by exploring her own vulnerabilities and acknowledging the impact of her past on her parenting style.

Peggy consciously chose to break the cycle of emotional suppression and embraced open communication with her children. She created a safe space for them to express their feelings without judgment. Drawing from her inner child's longing for validation, she made it a priority to affirm her children's emotions, fostering a sense of emotional security. Recognizing the importance of play and creativity, Peggy incorporated joyful activities into their daily routine, infusing the household with a sense of lightness and exploration.

Through self-reflection and intentional choices, Peggy not only nurtured her children's well-being but also embarked on her own healing journey. By understanding and reparenting her inner child, she broke free from generational patterns, fostering a home where love, understanding, and conscious presence thrived.

Dalton's Parenting Evolution

Dalton, a father of three in his early forties, underwent a profound transformation in his parenting approach by exploring the nuances of his inner child. Growing up in an environment where achievements were prioritized over emotions, Dalton realized the impact on his own parenting tendencies. Wanting to break the cycle of performance-driven expectations, he sought to consciously parent his children.

Dalton began by reflecting on his own inner child's desire for acknowledgment and support. He actively listened to his children, valuing their emotions and experiences beyond academic achievements. By sharing his own vulnerabilities and challenges, Dalton created a space for open dialogue within the family. He embraced the concept of playfulness, incorporating laughter and joy into their daily interactions, allowing his children to experience the carefree spirit of childhood.

In breaking free from the pressure-driven model he experienced growing up, Dalton encouraged his children to pursue their passions and interests authentically. Through this conscious shift, he not only fostered their individual growth but also forged a deeper connection with each child. Dalton's journey exemplifies how embracing and reparenting one's inner child can lead to positive changes in parenting dynamics, creating an environment of love, understanding, and conscious nurturing.

Healing Together

Diving into inner child work with your family and loved ones can be a seriously empowering thing for all involved. It's an awesome adventure that can seriously level up your connections and emotional vibes. Trust me, the benefits are worth the ride, setting the stage for healthier family vibes.

So, first off, imagine getting into each person's inner child world. It's like discovering a treasure trove of understanding, compassion, and resilience within your family. And guess what? One major perk is cranking up the empathy and communication game. When you explore everyone's inner child experiences, it's like unlocking secret codes to why people act the way they do. This newfound understanding becomes this magical bridge for talks where feelings and needs get spelled out crystal clear.

Now, the game-changer? Breaking those generational patterns. Families tend to pass down habits and beliefs like heirlooms. Inner child work is like hitting pause, spotting those patterns, and deciding, "You know what? Let's break free from this cycle." It's not just about individual healing; it's about creating a family space that's all about nurturing and lifting each other up.

Doing inner child work as a family creates this sense of unity and growth. It's like a group expedition where everyone's got each other's backs in their personal healing journey. This shared experience builds bonds that are all about realness, opening up, and having each other's six, making your family super resilient in tackling whatever life throws your way.

Oh, and get this—inner child work turns your family into emotional intelligence champs. As everyone tunes into their own and each other's emotions, it's like creating this space where feelings get the green light without any judgy vibes. This emotional awareness isn't just about understanding; it's a ninja move for handling conflicts, building trust, and turning your family vibes into a positive emotional fiesta.

In a nutshell, taking on inner child work with your family is like giving it a VIP ticket to emotional harmony. It's an investment in a family dynamic that's not just connected but super empathetic and resilient. Everyone gets to feel seen, heard and cheered on in their journey of healing and growth. Now, that's what I call a squad goal!

Want some cool activities that can bring your family together and spark that collective healing vibe? Ever tried a Family Storytelling Circle? Picture a cozy space where everyone takes turns sharing little tales from their childhood. It's not just about the stories; it's about embracing openness and vulnerability, creating this awesome connection through shared narratives.

Now, how about expressing your inner child through art? Imagine a chill art session where you and your family get creative—drawing, painting, whatever feels right. The focus? Bringing those childhood emotions and memories to life on canvas. Afterward, you can chat about the artwork, digging into those individual and collective healing vibes.

Feeling a bit zen? Give family meditation or mindfulness a shot. The whole crew engaging in a guided meditation, soaking up that emotional awareness and living in the moment. It's like a mini-retreat, letting everyone reflect on their emotions and sensations, creating this collective calm and self-awareness.

Ready for something visually cool? Try the generational family tree exercise. It's not your typical family tree—this one dives into emotional stuff too. Names and relationships? Check. But also emotional characteristics and experiences passed down through the generations. It's a visual journey that can help you spot patterns and chat about breaking those generational cycles for some sweet collective healing.

And how about an Affirmation Circle? Picture your family forming a circle, taking turns tossing out positive vibes and words of encouragement. It's all about creating this super supportive and uplifting vibe, making a collective promise to boost each other up. Share those qualities or strengths you love in one another—it's like a love fest that leaves everyone feeling pretty awesome.

The key to collective healing activities is creating an environment of trust, openness, and mutual respect. Tailor these exercises to fit the unique dynamics of your family, allowing each member to contribute to the healing process in a way that feels comfortable and meaningful for them. Let's read about how two families found their way through healing together.

The Johnson Family's Journey to Healing

The Johnson family, comprised of parents David and Rachel and their two teenage children, embarked on a transformative journey of healing together. Recognizing patterns of communication breakdown and unresolved emotional wounds, the family decided to engage in collective therapy and inner child work.

Through guided family therapy sessions, each member explored their inner child experiences, sharing stories, fears, and desires. The process allowed the family to develop a deeper understanding of each other's perspectives and cultivate empathy. They learned to communicate openly, expressing their needs and fears in a safe and supportive environment.

As the family continued their healing journey, they implemented new communication strategies and rituals that promoted emotional well-being. Regular family check-ins became a norm, providing an opportunity for each member to express their feelings and discuss any concerns. The Johnsons discovered shared values and strengths, creating a foundation for a more cohesive and resilient family unit.

Over time, the Johnson family witnessed a profound transformation. The healing journey not only repaired past wounds but also strengthened their bonds. The once-strained relationships flourished into a supportive and nurturing family dynamic, fostering an environment where each member felt seen, heard, and valued.

The Garcia Couple's Path to Reconnection

Maria and Javier Garcia, a married couple facing challenges in their relationship, decided to embark on a joint healing journey. Recognizing the impact of their individual childhood experiences on their marriage, they sought couples therapy with a focus on inner child work.

In therapy, Maria and Javier explored their inner child narratives, uncovering patterns of behavior and communication rooted in past experiences. Through guided exercises and open dialogue, they gained insight into each other's emotional landscapes, fostering a newfound empathy and understanding.

As the couple continued their healing process, they implemented intentional practices to nurture their relationship. Regular date nights became a priority, allowing them to reconnect and create positive memories together. The Garcias also developed rituals that honored their individual and shared values, fostering a sense of unity.

Their commitment to healing together led to a revitalized connection. Maria and Javier experienced a renewed sense of love and partnership, breaking free from destructive patterns. The healing journey not only revitalized their marriage but also served as a testament to the transformative power of shared inner child work in couples therapy.

Integrating the Inner Child into Adult Life

♥

The Balance of Play and Responsibility

Navigating the delicate balance between nurturing your inner child and navigating the responsibilities that come with adulting is a bit like walking a tightrope, but let me tell you, the effort is absolutely worth it for the sake of cultivating a well-rounded and emotionally healthy life.

Let's talk about that inner child of yours, shall we? That whimsical, creative, and endlessly curious part of you is akin to a secret sauce, and its potential to infuse vibrancy into your adult life is truly remarkable. Whether it's through engaging in hobbies that light up your passions, diving into creative pursuits that let your imagination run wild, or simply taking a moment to unwind and chill, your inner child is not just about having a good time—it's a profound source of stress relief, an energizing force that gives you that extra boost precisely when adulting starts to feel a bit overwhelming. Embracing this playful essence within you is like tapping into an everlasting reservoir of positivity and rejuvenation. So, go ahead, let that inner child of yours shine, and watch how it transforms your adulting experience into a more colorful and joy-filled journey.

Now, here's the essential trick: finding that perfect balance. It's akin to orchestrating playdates for your inner child while ensuring that your adult responsibilities don't feel neglected in the process. I get it, adulting is an inevitable part of life, and escaping its grasp is not really an option. However, what you can do is create a harmonious blend of playfulness that seamlessly integrates into your grown-up life.

Think of it as crafting a schedule that not only tackles your work deadlines, pays the bills, and takes care of all those adulting essentials but also carves out dedicated moments for your inner child to shine. It's about setting aside time for those hobbies that bring you genuine joy, engaging in creative pursuits that allow your imagination to flourish, and incorporating leisure activities that act as a breath of fresh air amid the responsibilities of adulthood.

It's about recognizing the value of both aspects of your life and understanding that they can coexist harmoniously. This delicate equilibrium is where the magic happens, where the responsibilities of adulthood don't become burdensome, and the playfulness of your inner child doesn't compromise your grown-up duties. So, in this intricate dance of life, embrace the challenge of balancing both worlds. Design a lifestyle that not only acknowledges the necessity of adult responsibilities but also honors the vitality of your inner child. The result? A life that is not only well-managed but also filled with a vibrant energy that stems from the perfect harmony of play and responsibility. It's about creating a narrative where your inner child doesn't just coexist with adulting but enhances the overall quality of your journey.

Quick tip time! Try sneaking in tiny doses of playfulness into your day:

1. Micro-Break Play: Take quick breaks for a doodle, a dance, or a playful stretch. It's like a burst of joy without wrecking your schedule.

2. Playful Morning Rituals: Kickstart your day with good vibes—upbeat music, a fun affirmation, or a playful breakfast ritual sets the mood.

3. Creative Commute: Turn your commute into a mini adventure. Podcasts, playlists, or a mental game can turn a routine drive into a playful journey.

4. Lunchtime Adventures: Lunch breaks are perfect for a playful escape. Take a walk, play a quick game, or try a new hobby—it's like a midday refresh.

5. Playful Workstation Setup: Jazz up your workspace with fun stuff. Colorful stationery, cute toys—anything that adds a touch of play to your workday.

6. Playful Mindfulness: Make mindfulness playful. Add some fun to deep breathing or meditation—it's like connecting with your inner child in a light and curious way.

7. Evening Playtime Rituals: Wind down with some playfulness. A quick game, a chat with loved ones, or a creative pursuit can turn your work-to-relax transition into a joyous ride.

Remember, you don't need hours; it's about sprinkling in those little moments. Adding playfulness brings joy, reduces stress, and boosts your mood. And guess what? It doesn't just stop there. Finding this balance? It's a recipe for better mental and emotional well-being. Your relationships get a glow-up, and life, in general, becomes a journey filled with joy, resilience, awesome connections, and deep fulfillment. Keep that playful spirit alive—it's the key to a life well-lived!

Embracing our emotions is a key aspect of a well-rounded and fulfilling life. It's not just about feeling the highs but also sailing through the lows with grace. When we give our emotions a nod, we open up this awesome space for personal growth, a deep dive into self-awareness, and this kick-butt resilience that helps us tackle whatever life throws at us.

Now, here are a few cool exercises that can be like your emotional superheroes – no capes, though. First up, mindful breathing – it's like giving your emotions a chill pill. Take slow, deep breaths, and let that calm wash over you. It's like hitting the emotional reset button. Or journaling – your feelings. Write it all down – the good, the bad, the messy. It's like your emotional confidant, helping you make sense of the emotional rollercoaster.

And who said you need words to express emotions? Enter Artistic expression – drawing, painting, sculpting. It's like an art party for your feelings. You don't need to be Picasso; it's about the feels, not the masterpiece. Or what about trying body scan meditation is next – it's like a spa day for your feelings. Start from your toes and work your way up, feeling where those emotions are sticking in your body. Consider what hurts, and where you're most tense – Are there any areas of your body that are particularly sensitive? It's like getting to know your emotions at their core.

Remember, it's not about bottling up emotions; it's about shaking hands with them. These exercises? They're like your emotional sidekicks, helping you surf through the feels with self-awareness, compassion, and unbeatable resilience. Now, ready for a couple of stories that spill the tea on the transformative magic of embracing emotions?

Navigating Shadows to Embrace Light:

Let me introduce you to Sam, a spirited individual navigating the unpredictable waters of early adulthood. Sam faced a cascade of challenges, starting with the sudden loss of a job that had been a source of stability. The abrupt departure of this professional anchor sent shockwaves through Sam's life, triggering a cascade of uncertainties and financial strain.

As if that weren't enough, a heart-wrenching breakup followed, adding emotional weight to an already tumultuous time. The breakup became a poignant punctuation mark in an unfolding narrative of change, leaving Sam to grapple with the dual specters of professional and personal upheaval.

In the face of these trials, Sam made a courageous decision to confront the emotional tempest head-on. Armed with a journal that would become a trusted confidant, Sam poured out feelings of sorrow, frustration, and the unnerving dance with the unknown. Friends became pillars of support, offering listening ears and comforting words, but the journey didn't end there.

Sam sought the guidance of a compassionate therapist, delving even deeper into the emotional labyrinth. Together, they explored the intricate layers of grief, self-doubt, and the myriad emotions that ebbed and flowed like the unpredictable currents of the sea. Through tear-stained pages and candid conversations, Sam discovered not only the strength to weather the storm but also a wellspring of resilience.

In the midst of this emotional storm, Sam found unexpected glimmers of hope within the darkest corners. The journey of self-discovery became a transformative expedition, unveiling not just emotional clarity but also equipping Sam with a robust toolkit. This toolkit wasn't a shield against future challenges but a compass to navigate life's unpredictable currents with grace, gratitude, and a newfound understanding of the resilient spirit within.

Illuminating Love Through Vulnerability:

Now, let's immerse ourselves in the intricacies of Susanne and Jamie's love story, a narrative that weathered the tests of time and distance. As they entered a season of physical separation and communication hurdles, challenges unfolded that tested the very fabric of their connection. The physical miles between them became symbolic of the emotional distance that threatened to wedge itself into the core of their relationship.

In the face of these challenges, Susanne and Jamie made a conscious decision to anchor their relationship in vulnerability. This choice, while brave, was not without its obstacles. The physical separation magnified the importance of effective communication, laying bare the need for emotional transparency.

Embracing inner child work, Susanne and Jamie opted for a path of open-hearted honesty. They recognized that sweeping emotions under the rug would only deepen the emotional chasm between them. In heartfelt conversations that laid bare fears and insecurities, they embarked on a profound exploration of each other's emotional landscapes. It was during these vulnerable moments that the power of inner child work became evident.

Susanne and Jamie delved into their pasts, uncovering the roots of their emotional responses and triggers. The process wasn't always easy; they confronted childhood wounds and learned to navigate each other's emotional sensitivities. Through this courageous dance with vulnerability, the couple not only bridged the physical gap but also forged a deeper emotional connection.

Inner child work became the bridge that spanned the emotional distance, allowing Susanne and Jamie to communicate with a level of understanding and compassion that transcended the physical miles. Their shared journey became a testament to the transformative nature of vulnerability and the profound impact of embracing their inner child selves. In revealing the beautifully imperfect depths of their souls to one another, Susanne and Jamie discovered that true intimacy blossoms not from a facade of perfection but from a shared willingness to navigate the complexities of their inner worlds with authenticity and love.

The Inner Child at Work

Ever noticed how the inner child isn't just hanging out in personal life but sneaks into the professional scene too? Yeah, it's the unsung hero shaping our work vibes – from sparking creativity to sometimes whispering insecurities in our ears.

But here's the deal: acknowledging the inner child at work isn't about reverting to kid mode at the office water cooler. It's more like diving into the emotional currents that shape our professional selves. Understanding this pint-sized influencer gives us a leg up in the workplace, adding a sprinkle of self-awareness, empathy, and emotional smarts to our toolkit.

Surprise, surprise – the workplace is like a playground for the inner child! When we build a culture that values creativity, encourages open chats, and throws in a dash of playfulness, we tap into the good vibes of our inner child. That means better collaboration and innovation on the job.

But wait – it's not all rainbows and sunshine. Dealing with the inner child's vulnerabilities is key to personal and professional growth. Think of it as a self-care party, boosting resilience and laying the groundwork for awesome work relationships. In a nutshell, the inner child's dance in the workplace is a mix of wide-eyed discovery and the wisdom that comes with self-awareness. Letting this side of ourselves shine makes our professional journey more authentic and balanced.

Ready to sprinkle some inner child magic in your career? Here are three cool strategies:

1. Playful Problem-Solving:

Tackle challenges with a playful twist. Imagine them as puzzles waiting to be cracked. Organize brainstorming sessions that welcome wild ideas. Let your imagination run wild – just like your inner child's.

2. Innovation in Daily Tasks:

Spice up routine tasks with a touch of innovation. Explore new approaches to the usual stuff. Try different tools or perspectives to make your work exciting. Turning the ordinary into a journey of discovery? That's the inner child's jam.

3. Collaborative Playground:

Make your workspace a collaborative haven. Celebrate diverse ideas. Set up platforms for open communication and idea-sharing. Acknowledge each team member's strengths – it's like creating a playground where everyone's voice adds to the team's awesomeness.

These strategies not only bring out your inner child's creativity in full force but also turn your workplace into a hub of innovation, exploration, and shared victories.

Now, let's peek into stories of people who let their inner child loose at work, not just bagging success but finding a deep sense of fulfillment and purpose in their careers. Ready for some workplace inspiration?

A Creative Leadership Exploration:

Jeanette, a seasoned marketing executive, embarked on a journey of self-discovery that unlocked her inner child's playful creativity. Recognizing the potential of imaginative thinking, she transformed her leadership style. Jeanette fostered an environment where brainstorming sessions felt like creative play, encouraging her team to explore unconventional ideas. This approach resulted in innovative marketing campaigns that not only resonated with audiences but also elevated Jeanette's reputation as a creative leader in the industry.

An Entrepreneurial Adventure:

Lamont, fueled by his inner child's adventurous spirit, ventured into entrepreneurship with a fresh perspective. Instead of viewing challenges as obstacles, he embraced them as exciting opportunities for growth. This mindset shift inspired Lamont to establish a tech start-up, where he introduced groundbreaking solutions to longstanding problems. His willingness to take calculated risks, driven by the enthusiasm of his inner child, positioned Lamont as a pioneering force in the entrepreneurial landscape, propelling his company to rapid success.

A Compassionate Leadership Evolution:

Marcy, a seasoned corporate manager, harnessed the power of empathy discovered through her inner child's reconnection. Viewing leadership through a compassionate lens, Marcy prioritized the well-being of her team. She created an inclusive work environment that mirrored the supportive dynamics of childhood friendships. By incorporating her inner child's qualities of kindness and understanding, Marcy's leadership style gained recognition. Her ascent to higher management roles was a testament to the transformative impact of infusing professional life with the principles of compassion inspired by her inner child.

Continuous Growth and Learning

Life is this ongoing story where we're constantly growing and discovering new things. Having a mindset of lifelong learning isn't just about your career – it's a nod to the fact that every twist and turn, whether a victory or a stumble, is a chance to learn, grow, and tackle challenges with the resilience and curiosity of our inner child.

Now, reconnecting with that inner child of yours – it's a journey full of exploration and play. But you'll need to entice that little you to come out and play. How about some artistic adventures? You could channel your inner Picasso by grabbing some paint, trying your hand at drawing, or even sculpting with clay. Create without judgment and let your imagination run wild!

And let's make exercise feel like play with playful movement practices. Think hula hooping, bouncing on a trampoline, or joining a dance class. Not only will these activities boost your physical well-being, but they'll also bring back the joy of moving freely. Or rekindle your love for the outdoors with exploration through nature. Take nature walks, go bird watching, or simply gaze at the stars. Connecting with nature in its simplest form lets your inner child marvel at the wonders around you.

And who could forget those game nights with friends and family? Bring them back with board games and puzzles. Not only will they tap into your competitive spirit, but they'll also infuse a lightheartedness reminiscent of childhood play. The main idea? Choose activities that bring joy and curiosity to your doorstep. Give yourself the freedom to explore and embrace the playfulness that's been waiting for its moment in the spotlight within your inner child.

Embark on the transformative journeys of individuals who embraced continuous learning. These narratives showcase the profound impact of acquiring new skills and hobbies on personal growth and fulfillment.

A Journey into Photography

Meet Pricilla, a spirited individual in her mid-thirties who discovered the transformative power of continuous learning through an unexpected passion – photography. She had always admired captivating images but never thought she could create them herself. One day, fueled by curiosity, Pricilla enrolled in a photography class at her local community center. Armed with a basic camera and a bucketload of enthusiasm, she dove headfirst into the world of composition, lighting, and storytelling through images.

As Pricilla navigated the challenges of understanding camera settings and framing shots, she found herself on a journey of self-discovery. Photography became more than just a hobby; it became a lens through which she viewed the world. Pricilla's newfound skill not only captured beautiful moments but also became a form of self-expression. The process of continuous learning, marked by trial and error, workshops, and endless hours of practicing, not only elevated her photography skills but also transformed her outlook on life. Through the lens of constant exploration, Pricilla discovered that learning is not confined to classrooms – it's an evolving adventure that shapes not just your skills but your entire perspective.

A Coding Odyssey

Now, let's meet Edward, a tech enthusiast with a passion for unraveling the mysteries of coding. Despite having a background in a non-tech field, Edward harbored a curiosity about the world of programming. One day, he decided to embark on an online coding journey. Armed with determination, countless online tutorials, and the support of coding communities, Edward began his odyssey into the world of Python, HTML, and CSS.

The path was not without its challenges. Edward faced bugs, errors, and moments of frustration that could have easily derailed his learning journey. However, he embraced each stumbling block as an opportunity to learn and grow. The online coding forums became his virtual classroom, providing guidance, feedback, and a sense of camaraderie with fellow learners. Through continuous learning, Edward not only grasped the intricacies of coding but also developed problem-solving skills and resilience.

What started as a quest to understand the fundamentals of coding turned into a transformative experience. Edward's newly acquired skills not only opened up opportunities for him in the tech industry but also instilled in him a profound belief in the limitless possibilities of continuous learning. His story is a testament to the idea that the journey of acquiring new skills is not just about mastering a craft but about evolving into a more adaptable, resilient, and open-minded version of oneself.

Living Authentically

Ever thought about living in sync with your true self? It's like rediscovering that playful, authentic spirit we had as kids – peeling back those layers of societal expectations and finding the genuine essence that defines us. When we embrace our inner child, it's all about honoring that curiosity, creativity, and pure joy that often takes a back seat when adulthood kicks in.

So, when we reconnect with our inner child, it's tapping into this well of authenticity that shapes our values and passions. It's saying, "Hey, my true self is all about those unfiltered expressions of my younger, uninhibited self." And guess what? This alignment brings a lightness to life – we get to navigate it with the same wonder and enthusiasm as a kid exploring a world bursting with possibilities.

Living authentically, hand in hand with our inner child, not only fills us with deep fulfillment but also makes us more resilient. Facing life's hurdles with the creativity and openness of our inner child gives us this unique perspective on challenges. It becomes our guiding force, steering us toward choices and paths that really resonate with who we are at our core. When we embrace our inner child, we open the door to a life that feels inherently meaningful, playful, and true to the authentic spirit within.

Now, imagine standing at life's crossroads. Honoring your inner child involves tuning in to those whispers of passion and joy. Think about decisions that align with the playfulness, creativity, and genuine curiosity that defined your younger self. Choose paths that bring that familiar excitement, letting your inner child dance freely in the tapestry of your life. It's like creating this perfect blend of responsibility and joy, paving a path that truly resonates with the playful heartbeat of your inner child.

Explore these stories of individuals who embraced their true selves, living authentically and unapologetically.

Unveiling Authenticity:

Julia's journey into authenticity unfolded as a tumultuous yet transformative adventure. The internal struggle was not just a battle against societal expectations but a deeply personal excavation of her true self. As a gifted artist with a flair for unconventional expressions, Julia found herself at odds with a world that often favored conformity over creativity.

The journey was marked by moments of vulnerability, where Julia faced the fear of judgment and rejection. Stepping into the spotlight with her genuine, unfiltered identity was akin to shedding layers of societal expectations that had become a heavy cloak. Battling self-doubt became a daily endeavor, with Julia questioning whether the world was ready for the raw authenticity she yearned to share.

Yet, amid these challenges, Julia's determination stood unwavering. The journey was a tapestry woven with acts of courage – showcasing her unconventional art, challenging norms, and embracing her unique perspectives. Through introspection and self-discovery, Julia found strength in vulnerability and authenticity. The process wasn't linear; it involved setbacks and triumphs, but each step forward echoed with the liberating melody of embracing one's true self. In the end, Julia's journey wasn't just about unveiling authenticity; it was a celebration of artistic expression, resilience, and the triumph of living life on her terms.

Marley's Journey to Self-Love:

Marley's path to authenticity was a courageous expedition into uncharted territory. Navigating a world that often seeks conformity, Marley faced the profound challenge of reconciling their non-conforming identity with societal expectations. Internal conflicts became a persistent companion, creating a complex inner landscape that yearned for acceptance.

The journey was not a linear progression but a series of peaks and valleys where Marley confronted the shadows of self-doubt and societal judgments. Prior to their transformative journey, there were moments when Marley felt invisible, their voice drowned in the cacophony of external expectations. The desire for genuine self-love became a beacon, guiding Marley through the labyrinth of self-discovery.

The transformation unfolded as Marley boldly chose to rewrite the narrative of their life. It was a process of shedding the layers of societal impositions, breaking free from the chains that confined their authentic self. Challenging the internal critic became an act of daily resilience, and fostering a compassionate relationship with themselves was the cornerstone of Marley's journey.

Through this intricate tapestry of self-love, Marley discovered that authenticity wasn't just about embracing their identity; it was a celebration of every aspect that made them uniquely and beautifully human. The journey wasn't without its challenges, but with each step towards self-acceptance, Marley forged a path illuminated by the profound authenticity that had been waiting to blossom. In choosing love over judgment, Marley's journey became an inspiration for others seeking the transformative power of self-acceptance and authenticity.

Celebrating the Journey

♥

As we stand at the threshold of concluding this transformative expedition, it's time to bask in the glow of our collective growth, honor the ongoing nature of inner child work, encourage the power of storytelling, explore the ripple effect of healing, and embark on final reflections and next steps.

Recognizing Your Transformation

Take a moment and reflect on the incredible journey you've been on with your inner child work. Consider the subtle shifts and monumental transformations that have unfolded, revealing practical insights and fostering emotional and spiritual growth. Think about the realizations born out of vulnerability and resilience, shaping the way you perceive yourself and others.

Those aha moments have likely influenced your decisions and the dynamics of your relationships. Delve into the emotional landscape you've traversed, from healing moments to self-discovery, noticing how each emotion has contributed to your evolving self. Your spiritual connection, nurtured through introspection and self-care, must have deepened your sense of purpose in tangible ways. Celebrate the resilience that carried you through challenges and recognizes that this commitment to inner child work is an ongoing journey, shaping your life with every intentional step forward.

As you reflect on these milestones, consider engaging in some reflective exercises like writing a heartfelt letter of gratitude to your inner child, exploring a timeline of significant moments, taking stock of your emotional landscape, starting a spiritual connection journal, and reflecting on the impact of your inner child work on your relationships. This offers a grounded approach to appreciate your journey, helping you uncover deeper insights and celebrate the progress you've made on your inner child work path.

Read this collection of heartfelt notes from readers who, like you, have embraced their inner child. These serve as a testament to the diverse and powerful ways in which inner child work can shape and elevate lives.

Emily's Take on Creativity

"When I tapped into my inner child, it was like unlocking this whole creative world I didn't even know existed. It felt like finding a box of crayons I'd forgotten about and adding a splash of color to the canvas of my life."

James' Thoughts on Healing:

"Playing my way to healing was unexpected and beautiful. It was like giving myself a permission slip to be a kid again, and in those playful moments, I found healing I didn't even know I needed. Laughter truly became my best medicine."

Sarah's Empowerment Journey:

"Choosing to be real is like having a secret superpower. Embracing my inner child wasn't just about being myself; it was about finding strength in it. It's funny how the world responds when you show up authentically—it's like I unlocked a whole new level of empowerment."

The Ongoing Journey

Embarking on the journey of inner child work is like nurturing the growth of a resilient plant, coaxing it into full bloom with patience and care. It's about embracing past hurts with empathy, offering solace to your younger self, and creating a nurturing space filled with self-love. Imagine understanding and becoming a compassionate companion, gently unraveling the threads of past experiences and decoding childhood memories to unveil patterns that shaped your responses. With this wisdom, you navigate your inner landscape, identifying triggers and making choices rooted in self-awareness and authenticity. As you lovingly nurture this growth, your inner world undergoes a beautiful transformation, blooming with self-love, emotional resilience, and a deep understanding of your intricate being—a testament to the enduring capacity for compassionate growth and healing within.

To maintain your connection with your inner child, consider simple daily check-ins, dedicating a few minutes to ask how they're feeling and what they need. Infuse creative rituals into your routine, whether through journaling, art, or meditation, as a way to nurture and connect with your inner child. Set aside intentional moments for inner child dates, engaging in activities that bring joy and playfulness, rekindling the connection with that carefree spirit within you.

Continuing inner child work is like uncovering a treasure chest for a richer life experience. It's an ongoing journey of self-discovery that adds layers of depth and understanding to your everyday encounters. By embracing this continuous exploration, you infuse your life with authenticity, wisdom, and a heightened sense of connection to both yourself and others. It's not just about healing the past; it's about weaving a tapestry of resilience and empathy, creating a life that's not just lived but truly experienced.

Sharing Your Story

Your journey is a one-of-a-kind adventure, and it holds the power to inspire others on their healing paths. Think about the impact storytelling can have as you share the lessons, triumphs, and challenges you've faced. When you open up and share your experiences, it creates a connection that goes beyond words – it becomes a source of strength and encouragement for those going through similar struggles. Your authentic storytelling is a compassionate way to build unity within a community of individuals navigating their unique journeys toward healing. It has the potential to inspire and cultivate a collective sense of resilience and growth.

When you start sharing your experiences, keep in mind that authenticity is key to crafting a compelling narrative. Being genuine in your storytelling, acknowledging both the highs and lows, invites readers into a deeper connection with your journey. Don't hold back on expressing the emotional nuances – the joys, struggles, and everything in between. Connecting emotionally allows you to empathize and helps others find aspects of your story that resonate with their own lives.

Encouraging empathy goes beyond just telling your tale. It's about recognizing and highlighting the universal aspects of the human experience that bring us together. Weave these common threads into your narrative to create a space for shared understanding and compassion. Your story becomes more than just a personal account; it becomes a vessel through which others can find echoes of their own experiences, fostering a sense of unity and collective strength. So, as you share your journey, embrace the authenticity of your story, dive into the emotional nuances, and cultivate empathy by connecting the shared threads of the human experience.

Witness how the vulnerability of one can ignite the spark of healing in others, creating a tapestry of collective resilience.

Inspiring Others to Seek Support:

Margo, a survivor of trauma, decided to share her healing journey through a blog where she openly discussed her therapy experiences, coping mechanisms, and the process of rebuilding her life. Her courageous storytelling resonated with readers who were facing similar challenges. Many reached out to express gratitude for Margo's openness, revealing that her story inspired them to seek professional help and embark on their paths to healing.

Fostering a Supportive Online Community:

Anthony, who battled addiction and successfully recovered, shared his story on social media, emphasizing the importance of community support. His narrative not only garnered positive responses but also led to the formation of an online support group. Individuals facing addiction found solace in Anthony's journey, and the community became a space for shared experiences, encouragement, and mutual understanding. Anthony's decision to share his healing journey resulted in the creation of a supportive digital community that continues to thrive.

The Ripple Effect of Healing

Individual healing has this incredible ripple effect that goes way beyond just our personal space. When people start on their healing journeys, it's like this magical transformation happens where they build up this extra dose of empathy, resilience, and compassion. And guess what? That strength becomes a guiding light for those around them.

When someone bravely opens up about their healing journey, it's like sending out this wave of encouragement. Others, seeing the power of resilience and self-discovery, might get that spark to start their healing adventures. Sharing both the tough moments and the victories breaks down the walls around mental health, making it okay to talk openly about personal growth.

And get this, as people heal individually, they often become these incredible sources of support in their communities. The compassion they've cultivated flows into acts of kindness, forming strong connections and a willingness to lend an ear without judgment. So, in a nutshell, individual healing is like stitching together a social fabric that's super empathetic and caring, creating a space where everyone's well-being is a top priority.

How about starting or joining support groups in your community? These gatherings are safe spaces where folks can share their healing stories, creating a supportive network that weaves into the community's fabric. Another idea – workshops and seminars. You could organize or be part of events that focus on emotional well-being, resilience, and healing. Sharing your insights can inspire others to kick off their journeys, and these events provide awesome tools and resources for growth.

And let's not forget acts of kindness! Sprinkle your community with little gestures – volunteering, helping out those in need, or just spreading good vibes. These small acts create a ripple effect, lifting individuals on their healing paths and fostering a sense of connection within the community.

Now, let's meet Rachel, a resilient soul whose healing journey ignited a wave of transformation within her community. Rachel openly shared her struggles with anxiety and depression, detailing the steps she took to reclaim her mental well-being. As she navigated the ups and downs of her healing process, Rachel's vulnerability resonated with those around her.

Inspired by Rachel's courage, a group of community members decided to form a support circle. Individuals facing similar mental health challenges found solace in sharing their experiences and learning from each other's coping mechanisms. The support group, initially a small gathering, grew into a flourishing community resource for emotional well-being.

Motivated by Rachel's example, the community organized workshops and seminars on mental health awareness. The collective understanding of the importance of emotional well-being permeated through various aspects of community life. Acts of kindness became a norm, creating a culture where individuals felt supported and understood.

Rachel's journey not only catalyzed her healing but became a catalyst for collective transformation. The community, inspired by her resilience, forged a path toward greater empathy, support, and openness about mental health. Through one person's journey, a community emerged stronger, more connected, and committed to nurturing the well-being of each member.

Final Reflections and Next Steps

Take away from this book the transformative lessons that revolve around your inner child's power – lessons grounded in compassion, understanding, and self-discovery. Let your inner child's strengths shine, set those healthy boundaries, and sprinkle a bit of playfulness into your everyday life. And hey, don't forget to recognize how past experiences might be shaping your present – we've got practical tools like visualization and therapeutic approaches to help you navigate and heal those bits.

Now, on your journey, keep in mind the magic of authentic communication, mastering your emotions, and building those deep, meaningful connections. The stories of resilience and growth shared here? They're not just stories – they're here to light a fire under you, inspiring your own self-discovery journey. This isn't the end, it's an open invitation to keep practicing self-compassion, empathy, and a commitment to growing as the amazing person you are. Let the wisdom of your inner child be your guide, turning your journey into a lifelong adventure of understanding, nurturing, and celebrating your authentic self.

As you wrap up the chapters of this book, take that wisdom of your inner child with you into the bright future ahead. Let compassion lead the way. Don't just see this as a conclusion – it's an invitation to embrace your strengths, set those boundaries, and keep that playful spirit alive every single day.

Living a life of emotional freedom is an ongoing journey, my friend. Approach it with openness, courage, and the understanding that every step gets you closer to a more authentic and fulfilling existence. Your emotional freedom isn't just a destination – it's a daily practice. Start now, and get ready to embrace the endless possibilities that come with honoring your truest self.

Conclusion

This isn't a wrap-up; it's just the beginning of something incredible. Carry the vibes of emotional freedom with you, and see each day as a chance for growth, connection, and pure joy. May your life shout out loud about the liberating power of embracing your inner child, building up that resilience, and just living life authentically. We've strolled through the intricate world of the inner child, peeling back layers and discovering the incredible transformation hidden in the corners of our past.

Hope is the cool breeze pushing us ahead, and your dedication to self-healing is the anchor keeping you steady in life's twists and turns. Remember, this journey isn't some final stop; it's an ongoing adventure – a promise to keep that flame of emotional freedom burning bright.

As you keep wandering through your inner world, let hope be your guide. Look at challenges as chances to grow, setbacks as mere stepping stones, and every emotion as a brushstroke adding to the masterpiece that is your life. You're a symbol of resilience, a living example of the amazing power of self-love and inner exploration. Take the lessons from this journey like a treasure chest of wisdom, unlocking its secrets whenever you need them.

In those quiet moments, chat with your inner child, showering love and assurance. When challenges show up, draw strength from that well of self-compassion you've carefully nurtured. You're the architect of your emotional world, and with each mindful step, you're crafting a life drenched in authenticity and purpose. Stepping out of these pages and into your future, may your days be filled with vibrant joy, sweet melodies of self-acceptance, and that profound peace that comes from embracing your inner child.

With heaps of gratitude for the journey we've shared and a heart brimming with hope, I'll catch you later. May your journey be sprinkled with joy, purpose, and a deepening bond with the lively spirit of your inner child. May laughter fill your days, fulfillment your heart and your path unfold with endless possibilities as you nurture the most authentic parts of yourself. Here's to the extraordinary adventure ahead – may it be as unique and beautiful as you are!